THE

HOLY

PRIESTHOOD

Volume 3

Ogden Kraut

Woman's Relationship to Priesthood

I [**Joseph Smith**] met the members of the "Female Relief Society," . . . and gave a lecture on the Priesthood, showing how the sisters would come in possession of the privileges, blessings and gifts of the Priesthood, and that the signs should follow them, . . . (DHC 4:602)

* * *

And for the information of all interested in this subject I [**John Taylor**] will say, it is not the calling of these sisters to hold the Priesthood, only in connection with their husbands, they being one with their husbands. (JD 21:367-368)

Pioneer Publishing
1067 E. Cumorah Dr
Genola, UT 84655
(801)754-5465
pioneerpublishing@msn.com
www.ogdenkraut.com

1st printing, 1994
2nd printing, 2005

PREFACE

This series of books on the Holy Priesthood would certainly not be complete without including one on the relationship of women to the Priesthood.

Since shortly before Joseph Smith's organization of the Relief Society in 1842 until the present time, the questions have been asked:

"Do women really hold the Priesthood?"

"What is their true relationship to Priesthood?"

"What did the early Church leaders think and teach about this subject?"

"Should LDS sisters ask to be given the Priesthood today?"

Answers to these questions range from one extreme to the other, with many variations in between. And, unfortunately, all the correct solutions will certainly not be found within the pages of this book, nor probably any other at present, since the Lord has not seen fit to give us sufficient definitive answers.

It is the intent of the author, however, to compile and present enough information so that the reader can at least be better informed about the issues involved, providing a better foundation and background on this controversial subject.

CONTENTS

Chapter 1

INTRODUCTION:
"IN THE BEGINNING. . ."

*While it is sadly true that it was a woman who brought sin into God's fair universe, it was likewise a woman who gave the world t.he Saviour from its sin. (Dr. Herbert Lockyer, "Introduction" to **All the Women in the Bible**)*

Was Mother Eve at fault for the sin and sorrow of this world? Did she bring disgrace and a curse upon her daughters so they would be deprived of Priest-hood? Or, was Eve a respectable and worthy woman entitled to the highest honors and blessings of the Holy Priesthood?

These are questions which have, for centuries, baffled preachers and lay believers alike. Even for many Mormons, who have additional knowledge and who are supposed to understand the order and rights of the Holy Priesthood, it has been a subject of great controversy and debate.

The Biblical account of Adam and Eve throws suspicion upon Eve's character and morality. Paul said, "Adam was not deceived, but the woman being deceived was in the transgression." (I Tim. 2:14) Then, of course, when Adam did the same thing, he became a transgressor on two counts: for partaking of the forbidden tree and for following the woman!

7

This is a peculiar part of Biblical history and doctrine because it is difficult to know which part is figurative and which is literal. It reminds the author of the school teacher who was boasting to her class of the power of mathematics in solving problems. One of the students responded with, "If by eating one apple, Mother Eve ruined the whole human family, what would an orchard full of apples do? An interesting sidelight is that the Bible doesn't even mention that Eve had an **apple**!

Many of the events surrounding the story of Adam and Eve have remained shrouded in mystery. Theo-logians, scholars, and scientists have entered the debating arena to battle out their theories as far as their imaginations could take them. It was not until light and knowledge were received from new revelation in these latter days that the darkness of ignorance and superstition was dispelled. As Brig-ham Young stated—

> *The very best of them would marvel why God suffered Lucifer or the serpent to tempt Mother Eve. That always has been a great mystery to the world, and is to this day, with the exception of the knowledge that has gone forth from the Lord through his Prophet Joseph. . . . (JD 6:144)*

Many religionists consider the actions of Adam and Eve to be a serious sin or transgression. Let us consider the definition of these two terms:

To transgress: to overstep or break (a law, commandment, etc.); to go beyond.

To sin: to break a religious law or moral principle; noun: an offense, misdemeanor, or fault.

In the case of our first parents, it was the **transgressing** of a lesser law (eating mortal food) in order to obey a higher law (procreating the earth with mortal children). Keeping both laws was an impossibility.

Brigham Young, because of his increased knowledge on the subject, was very lenient and understanding toward Adam and Eve, especially the latter:

Some may regret that our first parents sinned. **This is nonsense.** *If we had been there, and they had not sinned, we should have sinned.* **I will not blame Adam or Eve.** *Why? because it was necessary that sin should enter into the world; no man could ever understand the principle of exaltation without its opposite; no one could ever receive an exaltation without being acquainted with its opposite.* **How did Adam and Eve sin? Did they come out in direct opposition to God and to His government? No.** *But they* **transgressed** *a command of the Lord, and through that transgression, sin came into the world. The Lord knew they would do this, and He had designed that they should. (JD 10:312)*

We also understand the earth, and the nature of the earth, and **why God permitted Mother Eve to partake of the forbidden fruit.** *We should not have been here today if she had not; we could never have possessed wisdom and intelligence if she had not done it. It was all in the economy of heaven, and we need not talk about it; it is all right.* **We should never blame Mother Eve, not the least.** *(JD 13:145)*

The Book of Mormon also promotes this more understanding approach:

*And now, behold, if Adam had not transgressed, he would not have fallen, but he would have remained in the garden of Eden. (Here Nephi is putting most of the blame on Adam, not Eve.) * * * And they would have no children; wherefore they would have remained in a state of innocence, having no joy, for they knew no* *misery; doing no good, for they knew no sin." (2 Nephi 2:22,23)*

Nephi then concludes with the positive result: "Adam fell that men might be. . . ." (v. 25) It might be said that Eve took the lead in the transgression, but Adam took the responsibility. Another mortal world began as Eve became "the mother of all living," to fulfill the great mission she was appointed to before coming to this world.

Further study will reveal the fact that Eve set the stage for the order, the pattern and the example for all her daughters. She was a perfect "helpmate," "comforter," and "companion" to her husband in all things.

If their "fall" had been such a terrible sin, then certainly Adam and Eve would not have been worthy of the rights and blessings of the Holy Priesthood. The Prophet Joseph Smith said:

> *The Priesthood was first given to Adam; he obtained the First Presidency, and held the keys of it from generation to generation. He obtained it in the Creation, before the world was formed, as in Genesis 1:26, 27, 28. He had dominion given him over every living creature. He is Michael the Archangel, spoken of in the Scriptures. Then to Noah, who is Gabriel: he stands next in authority to Adam in the Priesthood; he was called of God to this office, and was the father of all living in this day, and to him was given the dominion. These men held keys first on earth, and then in heaven. (TPJS, p. 157)*

This clearly establishes that Adam was called to Priesthood obligations in the pre-mortal world, and he was not ignorant of his mission and responsibilities on earth. The same would apply to Eve as well.

Chapter 2

ALL ABOUT EVE

The Identity of Eve

The scriptures use three different terminologies when referring to Eve:

(1) One was "**Woman** because she was taken out of Man" (Gen. 2:23)—which was more of a generic designation because of her relationship with **Adam**. (2) Both Adam and Eve were collectively called Adam: "Male and female created he them; . . . and called their name Adam." (Gen. 5:2) —which refers more to "Adam's family"; they were an eternal unit of "one flesh". (3) Then again we read that Adam "called his wife's name Eve, because she was the mother of all living." (Gen 3:20) This was her designated work and mission—giving her life for her posterity.

Naturally, several "firsts" applied to our Mother Eve:

1. She was the first woman to live on the earth. She came as a complete and orderly woman with a special mission to perform. She did not come to earth as a child, a daughter, or a maiden, but as a married woman.

2. Eve was the first woman to be called a "wife". She was to fulfill a most important role with Adam. George Herbert

noted that "the man was dust refined, but the woman was dust double refined." (**All the Women in the Bible**, p. 56) She was to be good for him—spiritually, intellectually and socially. He could not be complete without her. In such a position she became equal to him.

3. She was the first female product of heaven—a display of beauty and perfection! Whatever may be said of loveliness and attractiveness, she reflected no artificial beauty.

4. Eve was the first sinless woman on earth. She had been holy in heaven, and walked and talked with her God. She knew the overall plan, and her mortal transgression had a divine purpose and good intent, and was a sacrifice that her children might come into mortality.

5. She was the first mother whose son was a murderer. She experienced the sorrow and grief of every mother who suffers because of the sins and wrongdoings of her sons and daughters. Justly or unjustly a mother suffers for her children. The mother of Jesus suffered over the horrid death of her innocent son. Mary Magdalene and other women suffered to see the cruelty heaped upon their husband.

6. Eve was the first to see the redemption of her children and the overcoming of the great serpent. She heard it said unto the old serpent, the devil, "I will put enmity between thee and the woman, and between thy seed and her seed; it shall bruise thy head, and thou shalt bruise his heel." (Gen. 3:15)

An impressive tribute was given to Eve and her daughters in the writings of Mosiah Hancock who saw in vision the pre-mortal world. When Lucifer rebelled, Mosiah saw that "no females took part against the Father and the Son, but all took sides in their favor." (Mosiah Hancock Journal, p. 71) That could not be said of all the males.

Another descriptive statement comes from the noted scholar and publisher, B. D. Zondervan, who wrote: "The description of creation (Gen. 1:26, 27) seems to imply that woman as the female counterpart to man is essential to the image of God." (**Zondervan Enc. of the Bible** 6:950)

This is obvious since it is written that "God created man in his own image, in the image of God created he him; male and female created he them." (Gen. 1:27) So, if God created them in His image as a man and a woman, the identity of God is also in the image of woman.

Woman was with man in the creation. Women have been at men's side sharing in their poverty, serving them in their sickness, and suffering with them in their wars. They were the last at the cross of crucifixion and the first at the sepulcher; then as if to show the honor given them in the heavens, they were the first to whom Christ appeared after his death.

Wise old Solomon beautifully described a good woman:

Who can find a virtuous woman? for her price is far above rubies. The heart of her husband doth safely trust in her, so that he shall have no need of spoil. She will do him good and not evil all the days of her life. *** Strength and honour are her clothing; and she shall rejoice in time to come. She openeth her mouth with wisdom; and in her tongue is the law of kindness. She looketh well to the ways of her household, and eateth not the bread of idleness. Her children arise up, and call her blessed; her husband also, and he praiseth her. *** Favour is deceitful, and beauty is vain; but a woman that feareth the Lord, she shall be praised." (Proverbs 31:10-12, 25-28, 30)

Certainly Eve was the epitome of all these virtues, and it can truly be said of her, "Many daughters have done virtuously, but thou excellest them all." (v. 29)

The Mission of Eve

A vital part of the mission of our Heavenly Father and Mother was that of continuing their posterity—first in spirit and then in the flesh. Through such procreation, they increase in dominion, power and glory. This concept is not understood by many outside of the Latter-day Saint Church; however, Herbert W. Armstrong wrote:

> *Consider why God created mankind in the first place! God is reproducing Himself through man! He is creating in man God's own perfect holy and righteous spiritual character! And that, in turn, is purposed to restore the Government of God over all the earth. And, further, to create billions of God beings to finish the creation of the vast unfinished universe!* (**Plain Truth**, Sept. 1980)

It is through women that this mission is continued, and since Eve was known as "the mother of all living," she was the "great-grandmother" of all nations, kindreds and peoples on this earth. While in mortality, children became her primary mission and glory, and childbearing was the fulfillment of her exclusive capability.

Among her mortal daughters, barrenness was considered a curse or a matter of incompleteness (i.e., see the accounts of Sarah in Gen. 16:1-2, Hannah in I Sam. 1:5-11, and Rachel in Gen. 30:1-4). It was to be the woman's natural responsibility to nurse, nurture, and care for her offspring. Her unique status in the home is indicated by the mention of the honor that should be given with a reward for long life in the land. Furthermore, there was a warning that no one else should "covet" her or take her from her special place.

Even though Eve had to bring mortal children into the world under a "curse" that would "greatly multiply thy sorrow and thy conception; in sorrow thou shalt bring forth children" (Gen. 3:16), she performed her mission honorably. This was not a complete sorrow, however, for she found joy in knowing she was obeying God's commandment and fulfilling her mission.

Every Latter-day Saint knows that children are a great blessing to their parents, as Erastus Snow declared:

> "Children are an heritage of the Lord, * * * and happy is the man that hath his quiver full of them." This doctrine permits the Latter-day Saints to fulfill the first great command given to Father Adam and Mother Eve. (JD 20:374)

If children are a heritage of the Lord, then Eve was fulfilling a mission for the Lord. She was performing the work assigned to her by the Lord, which is the work of the Kingdom. Jesus said:

> Suffer the little children to come unto me, and forbid them not; for of such is the kingdom of God. (Mark 10:14)

Along with her responsibility to have and raise children, Eve's mission, as well as that of her mortal daughters, includes an obligation to be an obedient and loving companion to her husband, for God had said, "I will make him an **help meet** for him" (Gen. 2:18), as defined below:

> . . . a help, a counterpart of himself, one formed from him, and a perfect resemblance of his person. If the word be rendered scrupulously literally, it signifies

one like, or as himself, standing opposite to or before him. And this implies that the woman was to be a perfect resemblance of the man, possessing neither inferiority nor superiority, but being in all things like and equal to himself. As man was made a social creature, it was not proper that he should be alone; for to be alone, i.e., without a matrimonial companion, was not good. Hence we find that celibacy in general is a thing that is not good, whether it be on the side of the man or of the woman. Men may, in opposition to the declaration of God, call this a state of excellence and a state of perfection; but let them remember that the word of God says the reverse. **(Adam Clarke's Bible Commentary** *1:45)*

Describing this part of Eve's mission further—

The Lord said that it was not good that man should be alone. He gave to him as a **helpmate** *one of His daughters by the name of Eve. This relationship was then instituted by the Almighty, and therefore a man and his wife should really become one; their interests, their labors should be blended; their responsibilities should be mutual; and in thus helping and aiding each other, they should train the posterity that God might give them in His fear and in the practice of righteousness, so that His rule and Kingdom might exist and prevail upon the earth. (Henry W. Naisbitt, JD 26:115, 1885)*

The Status of Eve

Man is not a self-contained individual, nor the whole and complete entity that he sometimes thinks he is. He cannot stand or be exalted by himself. That is why God said at the beginning that He would make a helpmeet for him. The marriage relationship is one of the most important and respected contracts in life. Marriage should not be just a temporal or passing arrangement, but an eternal covenant. It has been called a principle, an ordinance, a doctrine and a law.

The subordinate role of woman to man in the marriage relationship appears to be the result of the Fall rather than from her creation. At that time there was instituted a division of labor and responsibility—with the woman being assigned to the domestic realm and the other labors consigned to the man. Eve's submissive role to Adam set a pattern and a law that was to govern the relationship between men and women on this earth. This so-called "secondary" status has been disputed by many women ever since, and seems to be contested today more than ever. However, there needs to be order and organization in all things, as we have been instructed in our dispensation:

> *The Father as Spokesman and Leader. The family, a group of intelligent beings, must be organized, else chaos results. Just as there is but one Priesthood, but many offices in it, so every member of the family circle has equal claims upon the blessings of the home, but is assigned different tasks in connection with family life. * * **
> There must be a presiding authority in the family. The father is the head or president, or spokesman of the family. This arrangement is of divine origin. It also conforms to physical and physiological laws under which humanity live. A home, as viewed by the Church, is composed of a family group, so organized as to be presided over by the father, under the authority and in the spirit of the Priesthood conferred upon him.*
> *The position which men occupy in the family, and especially those who hold the Melchizedek Priesthood, is one of first importance and should be clearly recognized and maintained in the order and with the authority which God conferred upon man in placing him at the head of his household. (**Priesthood and Church Government,** Widtsoe, p. 81)*

Thus this type of family organization originated with Adam and Eve—with Adam designed to be the leader and ruler. Dr. Rodney Turner, BYU professor and author, elaborates on this:

*The significance of the woman being named Eve is heightened by the fact that it was done, not by God, but by her husband. Adam had been made lord of all creation—guardian over the entire earth and every living thing thereon. In connection with this appointment, he named all things. **The right to name connotes the right to rule.** In naming his wife, Adam became—by divine appointment—her steward. And in accepting that name, Eve acknowledged Adam's position and submitted herself to the righteous leadership of the holy priesthood. A similar commitment is inferred in those marriages where the woman takes upon herself the name the man gives her—his name. (**Women and the Priesthood**, Turner, p. 41)*

In many ways, however, the status of a husband-and-wife relationship can be compared to a pioneer handcart.

Each wheel is necessary to the function of the cart. The unit of the husband-and-wife team is necessary for the progress of the family. Each wheel serves the other; and as the movement of one wheel depends on the same movement of the other, so does a wife depend on the progress of her husband.

She must be a helpmeet to him for her own benefit as well as his. If one wheel goes slower than the other, or even stops, then the cart just goes around in circles. The wheel must be either "repaired" or "replaced" in order for the cart to continue going in the right direction.

But the principle of free agency still plays an important part in this husband-and-wife relationship. Joseph F. Smith described:

> *We have got to learn to stand or fall for ourselves, male and female. It is true that we are taught in the principles of the Gospel that man is the head of the woman, and Christ is the head of the man; and according to the order that is established in the kingdom of God, it is the duty of the man to follow Christ, and it is the duty of the woman to follow the man in Christ, not out of him. But has not a woman the same volition that the man has? Can she not follow or disobey the man as he can follow or disobey Christ? Certainly she can; she is responsible for her acts, and must answer for them. She is endowed with intelligence and judgment, and **will stand upon her own merits** as much so as the man. (JD 16:247)*

The status of a woman is beautifully described by Matthew Henry when he discussed the figurative creation of woman from the rib of man:

> *The woman was made of a rib out of the side of Adam; not made out of his head to rule over him, nor out of his feet to be trampled upon by him, but out of his side to be equal with him, under his arm to be protected, and near his heart to be loved. (**Matthew Henry's Commentary**, 1:20)*

In the very beginning it is written that man and woman enjoyed the immediate presence of God. They were, so to speak, still living at home. The man did not try to impose his will over the woman, but each looked upon the other as a counterpart—like a pair of scissors that needed each other to properly function.

The objective then, as a mortal couple, is to regain the same position and status that Adam and Eve had before the fall. It can be done only by following the laws which were given to Adam and Eve while they were in the Garden of Eden, for the promise was that "they shall be as Gods, knowing good and evil." To further illustrate:

*The word of God abideth forever. God made the woman for the man, and thus he has shown us that every son of Adam should be united to a daughter of Eve to the end of the world. (See I Cor. vii.) God made the woman out of the man, to intimate that the closest union, and the most affectionate attachment, should subsist in the matrimonial connection, so that the man should ever consider and treat the woman as a part of himself: and as no one ever hated his own flesh, but nourishes and supports it, so should a man deal with his wife; and on the other hand the woman should consider that the man was not made for her, but that she was made for the man, and derived, under God, her being from him; therefore the wife should see that she reverence her husband (Eph. v. 33). The 23rd and 24th verses contain the very words of the marriage ceremony: This is flesh of my flesh, and bone of my bone, therefore shall a man cleave unto his wife, and they two shall be one flesh. How happy must such a state be where God's institution is properly regarded, where the parties are married, as the apostle expresses it, in the Lord; where each, by acts of the tenderest kindness, lives only to prevent the wishes and contribute in every possible way to the comfort and happiness of the other! Marriage might still be what it was in its original institution, pure and suitable; and in its first exercise, affectionate and happy. (**Adam Clarke's Commentary**, 1:46)*

The Priesthood Rights of Eve

In the divine order woman was given to man, not man to the woman. Eve was given to Adam to be his helpmeet and companion, and share in the building of His kingdom in a way that he could not do alone. There was an order established and one had to be the head, yet they shared all things in common.

Most of Christianity look upon Eve as a weak and sinful vessel, through whom the old serpent, the devil had his greatest victory. The Mormons, on the other hand, hold Eve in the greatest respect, if not reverence. Over a century ago, Edward Tullidge wrote:

*The fall is simple. Our immortal parents came down to fall; came down to transgress the laws of immortality; came down to give birth to mortal tabernacles for a world of spirits. * * * Eve, then, came down to be the mother of a world. Glorious Mother, capable of dying at the very beginning to give life to her offspring, that through mortality the eternal life of the Gods might be given her sons and daughters. Motherhood the same from the beginning even to the end! The love of motherhood passing all understanding! Thus read our Mormon sisters of the fall of their mother. (**Women of Mormondom**, Tullidge, pp. 197-98)*

With Eve's knowledge of proper family organization, she certainly recognized and respected Adam's presiding Priesthood authority as well as her rights and privileges connected thereto:

There is no higher authority in matters relating to the family organization, and especially when that organization is presided over by one holding the Higher Priesthood, than that of the father. This authority is time honored, and among the people of God in all dispensations it has been highly respected and often *emphasized by the teachings of the Prophets who were inspired of God. The Patriarchal order is of divine origin, and will continue throughout time and eternity. There is then a particular reason why men, women and children should understand this order and this authority in the households of the people of God, and seek to make it what God intended it to be, a qualification and preparation for the highest exaltation for His children. **In the home the presiding authority is always vested in the father**, and in all home affairs and family matters there is no other authority paramount. (**Juve. Instr.**, March 1, 1902)*

Regarding Eve's high and exalted position, it is interesting to compare two accounts of a vision experienced by Joseph Smith along with Zebedee Coltrin and Oliver Cowdery or Sidney Rigdon. In one report by Zebedee Coltrin in **The School of the Prophets**, the two heavenly beings are identified as **Adam and Eve**; in the other one, recorded by Abraham H. Cannon, the same two beings are referred to as the **Father and Mother**, the capital letters signifying deity.

Once after returning from a mission, he [Coltrin] met Bro. Joseph in Kirtland, who asked him if he did not wish to go with him to a conference at New Portage. The party consisted of Prests. Joseph Smith, Sidney Rigdon, Oliver Cowdry [sic] [O. Cowdery was not mentioned in the other account.) and myself [Coltrin]. Next morning at New Portage, he [Coltrin] noticed that Joseph seemed to have a far off look in his eyes, or was looking at a distance, and presently he, Joseph, stepped between Brothers Cowdry [sic], and Coltrin and taking them by the arm, said, "lets take a walk." They went to a place where there was beautiful grass, and grapevines and swamp-beech interlaced. President Joseph Smith than [sic] said, "Let us pray." They all three prayed in turn—Joseph, Oliver, and Zebedee. Brother Joseph than [sic] said, "now brethren we will see some visions." Joseph lay down on the ground on his back and stretched out his arms and the *two brethren lay on them. The heavens gradually opened, and they saw a golden throne, on a circular foundation, something like a light house, and on the throne were two aged personages, having white hair, and clothed in white garments. They were the two most beautiful and perfect specimens of mankind he ever saw. Joseph said, They are our first parents, **Adam and Eve**. Adam was a large broadshouldered man, and Eve as a woman, was large in proportion. (Located in LDS Church Hist. Dept. Archives, under the date of Oct. 11, 1883, as reprinted in **S.L. School of the Prophets Minute Book, 1883**, Pioneer Press, p. 64)*

* * *

*Pres. Petersen told of an incident which he often heard Zebedee Coltrin relate. One day the Prophet Joseph Smith asked him [Zebedee Coltrin] and Sidney Rigdon to accompany him into the woods to pray. When they had reached a secluded spot, Joseph laid down on his back and stretched out his arms. He told the brethren to lie one on each arm and then shut their eyes. After they had prayed, he told them to open their eyes. They did so and they saw a brilliant light surrounding a pedestal which seemed to rest on the earth. They closed their eyes and again prayed. They then saw, on opening them, the **Father** seated upon a throne; they prayed again and on looking saw the **Mother** also; after praying and looking the fourth time, they saw the Savior added to the group. He had auburn brown, rather long, wavy hair and appeared quite young. (**Abraham H. Cannon Jrnl.** Aug. 25, 1890, located in Archives and Manuscripts, Special Collections H.B. Lee Library, BYU)*

Since Adam and Eve were seated upon a "golden throne" and held such exalted positions, it is evident that they have reached an extremely high place in the realm of the Gods, involving the possession of Priesthood powers. Thus, Eve must have shared in all the blessings, rights and privileges that can be offered by the Holy Priesthood.

Chapter 3

ANCIENT MATRIARCHS
OF THE SCRIPTURES

It takes only a quick look through the Bible to see that other noble women besides Eve were worthy to receive the blessings of the Priesthood. Their examples of bravery, intelligence, and righteousness prove that they are entitled to these blessings as much as the men.

Woman has many striking examples of her influence and acts in the history of religious empire-founding. Miriam charmed the congregation of Israel with her songs, and strengthened her brother Moses' power by her prophesies; Esther rendered the captivity of her people lighter by her mediation; Judith delivered her nation from the Assyrian captain; the two Marys and Martha seemed to have understood Jesus better than did his apostles even, and they saw first their risen Lord; St. Helena did much to make her son, Constantine, the imperial champion of Christianity; perchance had there been no Cadijah the world would never have known a Mohammed; the Catholic Church has been more potent through the sisters of its various orders; and the examples which the Mormon sisterhood have given are almost as striking as those of the sisters of that church. (**Women of Mormondom**, *Tullidge, p. 277*)

24

Women of the Old Testament

Old Testament writers proclaim high respect for woman's rights and blessings, especially in her religious life. In some cases her spirituality, faith and perseverance far excelled those of her male counterpart. Some women were even elevated to the status of "prophetess". There was Huldah, who lived at the time of Isaiah (2 Kings 22:14; 2 Chron. 34:22), Miriam, the sister of Moses (Ex. 15:20), Deborah, one of the judges in Israel (Judges 4:4), the wife of Isaiah (Isa. 8:3), and even a "false prophetess" named Noadiah (Neh. 6:14).

Regarding Huldah, Orson Pratt in 1859 referred to her great gift and power of prophecy:

> *The history of the inspired writings anterior to the Babylonish captivity is very brief. The number of copies were very few. In the days of Josiah, all of the Jews seem to have been destitute of a copy of the law. During the reign of that king, in repairing the house of the Lord, a copy of the book of the law was found; and when presented to the king, he sent five messengers to Huldah, the prophetess, saying, "Go, inquire of the Lord for me, and for them that are left in Israel and in Judah, concerning the words of the book that is found." The messengers returned and reported to the king that the book found was indeed a Divine revelation, and the king caused all the inhabitants of Jerusalem to be assembled to hear the words of the book. (See 2 Chron. 34.)*
>
> *For a long period previous to finding the book, the Jews had been ignorant of the Scriptures, and had fallen into the grossest idolatry. A new revelation through the prophetess Huldah seems to have been sufficient to convince the king and all Israel of the divinity of the book. They must have been inclined, in that age of the world, to believe the history of the servants of God more than in this age; for now the people generally require a vast amount of evidence. The testimony of a dozen witnesses is scarcely regarded.*

> *I have already observed, through the persecutions raised against the house of Israel, their books were destroyed; yes, even the tables of stone, for some reason, were taken from them, and all Israel were left without even a copy of the law, until accidentally they happened to find one that had been hid in the house of the Lord, as I have already named; and they were so ignorant with regard to this copy that they were obliged to send for Huldah, one of the prophetesses in Israel, to inquire of the Lord to know if it really was his word. They found a book, but they did not know whether it was true or false; and they thought it important that it should be determined by the immediate word of God. (JD 7:23-24)*

If the Lord worked through women anciently, why would it not be reasonable for Him to do so now? Certainly their basic characteristics and desires are similar—as well as the universal need for divine guidance.

In ancient Israel selected women could share in the privileges and opportunities of royalty. Whatever the king enjoyed, she could enjoy; wherever he went, she could go; whatever freedoms were had in that kingdom, she also had. Hers was an enviable social status in comparison to that of other nations. Often these women in Israel were endowed by God with special insights, spiritual gifts and the power to change the course of history. No one has read the story of Esther without being impressed with her courage and mission and the effect she had on the House of Judah. Henry Haley comments on her life:

> *Esther, it seems, made possible the work of Nehemiah. Her marriage to the King must have given Jews great prestige. It is impossible to guess what might have happened to the Hebrew nation had there been no Esther. Except for her, Jerusalem might never have been re-built, and there might have been a different story to tell to all future ages.*

*This book of Esther is about a very important histori-cal event, not just a story to point a moral: The Hebrew nation's deliverance from annihilation in the days fol-lowing the Babylonian captivity. * * **

This beautiful Jewish girl of the long ago, though she herself may not have known it, yet played her part in paving the way for the coming of the world's Saviour. (**Haley's Bible Handbook**, *p. 222*)

During the 400 years of history that are missing between the Old and New Testaments, the scribes of the Jewish nation wrote about numerous events and philosophies. Heroic accounts of women were found in the **Apocrypha**—women who exhibited many noble virtues such as faith, patriotism, loyalty and piety.

One of these heroines was Judith, the widow who fast-ed through all the assigned sabbaths, new moons and solemn days. It is written that "she was also of a goodly countenance, and very beautiful to behold;" also she possessed much gold, silver and lands, yet she was not proud or vain. And besides "there was none that gave her an ill word; for she feared God greatly." (See Judith 8:8.) She was of such wisdom and spirituality that she spoke counsel to the governors of the land when they were about to be invaded by the Assyrians. Then she went to pray. She covered herself in sackcloth and ashes, and in her prayer she acknowledged the power of God in pro-tecting the people:

They are exalted with horse and man; they glory in the strength of their footmen; they trust in shield, and spear, and bow, and sling; and know not that thou art the Lord that breakest the battles. . . . (Judith 9:7)

For thy power standeth not in multitudes, nor thy might in strong men; for thou art a God of the afflicted, an helper of the oppressed, an upholder of the weak, a protector of the forlorn, a saviour of them that are *without hope. * * * Make every nation and tribe to acknowledge that thou art the God of all power and might, and that there is none other that protecteth the people of Israel but thou. (Judith 8:7,11)*

Here was a woman acting as an example for men who held the Priesthood. Like Joan of Arc, Judith went through the camps of soldiers and met with the army leaders to explain what God wanted.

Another remarkable and impressive story from the **Apocrypha** is the account of seven men and their mother who were taken before the king to be tried and tested by whip and fire. The king wanted them to forsake their religion and covenants, but as one of the sons said, "We are ready to die rather than to transgress the laws of our fathers." One by one they cut out their tongues, scalped them, chopped their arms and legs off and fried them on red hot pans. Even the king and his servants marvelled at their courage. One of the young men said, "Thou like a fury takest us out of this present life, but the King of the world shall raise us up, . . ." Another said, "It is good being put to death by men, to look for hope from God to be raised up again by Him." When her last son was brought forward, the mother encouraged him by saying, "Fear not this tormentor, but, being worthy of thy brethren, take thy death, that I may receive thee again in mercy with thy brethren." Then he, too, was put to death. The mother watched the death of all of her sons, and it is written:

But the mother was marvellous above all, and worthy of honourable memory: for when she saw her seven sons slain within the space of one day, she bare it with a good courage, because of the hope that she had in the Lord. Yea, she exhorted every one of them in her own language, filled with courageous spirits; and stirring up her womanish thoughts with a manly stomach, she said unto them, "I cannot tell how ye came into my womb, for I neither gave you breath nor life. . . but doubtless the Creator of the world, who formed the generation of man, and found out the beginning of all things will also of his own mercy give you breath and life again, as ye now regard not your own selves for His law's sake." (II Maccabees 7:20-23)

Then the faithful and courageous mother, while praising God, followed her sons in an honorable death.

What are the requirements to be worthy of receiving Priesthood blessings? Is it righteousness? the love of God? willingness to lay down one's life for the truth? Are there any of these qualifications that women have not displayed in their lives? Where the Holy Priesthood is found, righteous qualities abound, and where those principles are not found, neither is the Priesthood. Many of the gifts of the spirit are enjoyed by those possessing the Priesthood, but they have also been enjoyed by deserving women.

Women of the New Testament

In the New Testament, stories of women were constantly intermingled with Christ and His ministry.

In the actual life of Jesus, specific women play an important role. Mention is made of Mary Magdalene, Mary the mother of James and Joseph, the other Mary, the mother of the sons of Zebedee as well as Mary and Martha. Much of Jesus' ministry was centered upon the needs and requests of women. One of Jesus' earliest acts of healing was the mother of Peter (Mark 1:29 ff.). In addition to the healing of the woman with the hemorrhage (Luke 8:43 ff.), there is recorded the raising from the dead the son of the widow of Nain (7:11-17), the healing of the daughter of the woman from Syro-phoenicia (Mark 7:24-30), and the raising of Lazarus in response to the pleas of Mary and Martha

*(John 11:17-43). At the same time, Jesus often addressed His teaching to women and used women as illustrations of spiritual truths: a woman loses a coin (Luke 17:35), at the well in Sychar it is a woman of questionable reputation who meets Jesus, and the questionable passage of John 7:53 - 8:11 centers upon a woman charged with the capital offense of adultery. Observe also that it is women who are specifically mentioned as following Jesus on His last journey to Jerusalem and His crucifixion (Matt. 27:55, 56); they were present at the scene of the crucifixion (Luke 23:49); they prepared the body with spices and ointments for burial and followed the body to the grave site (Matt. 27:61; Luke 23:55, 56); on the morning of the resurrection they were first at the tomb (Matt 28:1; Mark 16:1; Luke 24:1; John 20:1); and they were the first to witness the risen Lord in His triumph over death (Matt. 28:9; Mark 16:9; John 20:14). (**Zondervan's Enc. of the Bible** 6:984)*

Paul recognized the useful and necessary labors of women in the Church. He began his letter to the Romans—

I commend unto you, Phebe, our sister, which is a servant of the church which is at Cenchrea: that ye receive her in the Lord, as becometh saints, and that ye assist her in whatsoever business she hath need of you: for she hath been a succourer of many, and of myself also. Greet Priscilla and Aquila, my helpers in Christ Jesus: Who have for my life laid down their own necks: unto whom not only I give thanks, but also all the churches of the Gentiles. (Romans 16:1-4)

Paul had an interesting experience when he went to Caesarea, and he wrote:

We entered into the house of Philip, the evangelist, which was one of the seven; and abode with him. And the same man had four daughters, virgins, which did prophesy. And as we tarried there many days, . . . (Acts 21:8-10)

Here were four girls who had the gift of prophecy, and although Paul remained in that house for "many days", he gives no mention of discouraging these girls in that high and holy gift. He does not condemn nor criticize them, indicating that the Lord must have been pleased with them as well. According to Paul, prophecy is the greatest of gifts, and it is evident that there were Biblical women called prophetesses to whom the Lord gave that gift.

But Paul did place particular restrictions on women in the church, and his views have brought him considerable reproach from today's more liberated women.

> *Let your women keep silence in the churches: for it is not permitted unto them to speak; but they are commanded to be under obedience, as also saith the law. And if they will learn anything, let them ask their husbands at home: for it is a shame for women to speak in the church. * * * Let all things be done decently and in order. (I Cor. 14:34, 35, 40)*

When Paul wrote to Timothy, he made some suggestions for men in the church, and in that same letter he also gave some advice to the women. These are not hard and fast laws of the church, but rather Paul's personal views:

> *Women adorn themselves in modest apparel, with shamefacedness and sobriety; not with broided hair, or gold, or pearls, or costly array; but (which becometh women professing godliness) with good works. Let the woman learn in silence with all subjection. But I suffer not a woman to teach, nor to usurp authority over the man, but to be in silence. * * * Notwithstanding she shall be saved in childbearing, if they continue in faith and charity and holiness with sobriety. (I Tim. 2:9-12, 15)*

Paul continued with other instructions to Timothy, such as, "Lay hands **suddenly** on no man. . . ." (Tim. 5:22), meaning that men should be selected carefully for ordinations and the Priesthood.

In Paul's letter to the Corinthian saints he also mentioned the marriage relationship, including a passage which is somewhat difficult to understand:

> *Let the husband render unto the wife due benevolence: and likewise also the wife unto the husband. The wife hath not power of her own body, but the husband: and likewise also the husband hath not power of his own body, but the wife. (I Cor. 7:3-4)*

Matthew Henry's **Bible Commentary** says this infers that "in the married state neither person has power over his own body, but has delivered it into the power of the other." (6:537) Adam Clarke's **Commentary** says it a little clearer: "Her person belongs to her husband; her husband's person belongs to her: neither of them has any authority to refuse what the other has a matrimonial right to demand." (6:221)

From these passages it is clear that men, even those with the Priesthood, have no power over their own bodies, but neither does she have power over hers—in a matrimonial sense. As a wife she becomes a part of him—"one flesh", which bears his burdens and enjoys his rights. Whatever he can claim for his own, it is also hers and vice versa. Whatever he achieves on earth or in heaven, she can share.

Peter (of whom Joseph Smith said, "Peter penned the most sublime language of any of the apostles." [TPJS, p. 301]) wrote similar suggestions to both men and women of the church in his day:

> *Likewise, ye wives, be in subjection to your own husbands; that, if any obey not the word, they also may without the word be won by the conversation of the wives;*

While they behold your chaste conversation coupled with fear.

Whose adorning let it not be that outward adorning of plaiting the hair, and of wearing of gold, or of putting on of apparel;

But let it be the hidden man of the heart, in that which is not corruptible, even the ornament of a meek and quiet spirit, which is in the sight of God of great price.

For after this manner in the old time the holy women also, who trusted in God, adorned themselves, being in subjection unto their own husbands:

Even as Sara obeyed Abraham, calling him lord: whose daughters ye are, as long as ye do well, and are not afraid with any amazement.

Likewise, ye husbands, dwell with them according to knowledge, giving honour unto the wife, as unto the weaker vessel, and as being heirs together of the grace of life; that your prayers be not hindered. (I Peter 3:1-7)

Mary, the mother of Jesus, was certainly an outstanding example of a noble and virtuous woman, but no mention is made of her taking part in the work of the ministry. This was a woman who was "found with child of the Holy Ghost" (Matt. 1:18), and "that which is conceived in her is of the Holy Ghost" (Matt. 1:20), and when an angel appeared to her, he said, "The Holy Ghost shall come upon thee, and the power of the Highest shall overshadow thee" (Luke 1:35). Yet, with all this Holy Ghost power and association, she never went out as a missionary nor is there any record of her holding an office in the Priesthood or being active in any of its councils. With all the references to Jesus being the "Son of God" and the "Son of the Highest", Mary was not even a member of the Sanhedrin nor was she ordained to the office of a Rabbi, nor any other Priesthood office.

Women of the Book of Mormon

Although the Book of Mormon contains very few passages about women directly, it is obvious that they, too, experienced the hardships and privations of traveling in the wilderness and across the ocean (as recorded in 1st Nephi); bore a great deal of the responsibility in setting up their households in the "new world"; and suffered from the pains and losses resulting from sickness and battle.

In an account recorded by Alma, he tells about the great faith of a Lamanite queen (wife of King Lamoni) and also the conversion of Abish, a Lamanite woman:

And it came to pass that after two days and two nights they were about to take his [King Lamoni's] body and lay it in a sepulchre, which they had made for the purpose of burying their dead.

Now the queen having heard of the fame of Ammon, therefore she sent and desired that he should come in unto her. And it came to pass that Ammon did as he was commanded, and went in unto the queen, and desired to know what she would that he should do.

And she said unto him: The servants of my husband have made it known unto me that thou art a prophet of a holy God, and that thou hast power to do many mighty works in his name; Therefore, if this is the case, I would that ye should go in and see my husband, for he has been laid upon his bed for the space of two days and two nights; and some say that he is not dead, but others say that he is dead and that he stinketh, and that he ought to be placed in the sepulchre; but as for myself, to me he doth not stink.

Now, this was what Ammon desired, for he knew that king Lamoni was under the power of God; he knew that the dark veil of unbelief was being cast away from his mind, and the light which did light up his mind, which was the light of the glory of God, which was a marvelous light of his goodness—yea, this light had

infused such joy into his soul, the cloud of darkness having been dispelled, and that the light of everlasting life
was lit up in his soul, yea, he knew that this had overcome his natural frame, and he was carried away in
God—

Therefore, what the queen desired of him was his only
desire. Therefore, he went in to see the king according as
the queen had desired him; and he saw the king, and he
knew that he was not dead.

And he said unto the queen: He is not dead, but he
sleepeth in God, and on the morrow he shall rise again;
therefore bury him not. And Ammon said unto her:
Believest thou this? And she said unto him: I have had
no witness save thy word, and the word of our servants;
nevertheless **I believe that it shall be according as
thou hast said.**

And Ammon said unto her: Blessed art thou because
of thy exceeding faith; I say unto thee, **woman, there
has not been such great faith among all the people
of the Nephites.**

And it came to pass that she watched over the bed of
her husband, from that time even until that time on the
morrow which Ammon had appointed that he should
rise.

And it came to pass that he arose, according to the
words of Ammon; and as he arose, he stretched forth his
hand unto the woman, and said: Blessed be the name of
God, and blessed art thou. For as sure as thou livest,
behold, I have seen my Redeemer; and he shall come
forth, and be born of a woman, and he shall redeem all
mankind who believe on his name.

Now, when he had said these words, his heart was
swollen within him, and he sunk again with joy; and the
queen also sunk down, being overpowered by the Spirit.

Now Ammon seeing the Spirit of the Lord poured out
according to his prayers upon the Lamanites, his
brethren, who had been the cause of so much mourning
among the Nephites, or among all the people of God
because of their iniquities and their traditions, he fell
upon his knees, and began to pour out his soul in
prayer and thanksgiving to God for what he had done

for his brethren; and he was also overpowered with joy; and thus they all three had sunk to the earth.

Now, when the servants of the king had seen that they had fallen, they also began to cry unto God, for the fear of the Lord had come upon them also, for it was they who had stood before the king and testified unto him concerning the great power of Ammon.

*And it came to pass that they did call on the name of the Lord, in their might, even until they had all fallen to the earth, save it were one of the Lamanitish women, whose name was **Abish, she having been converted unto the Lord for many years, on account of a remarkable vision of her father—***

Thus, having been converted to the Lord, and never having made it known, therefore, when she saw that all the servants of Lamoni had fallen to the earth, and also her mistress, the queen, and the king, and Ammon lay prostrate upon the earth, she knew that it was the power of God; and supposing that this opportunity, by making known unto the people what had happened among them, that by beholding this scene it would cause them to believe in the power of God, therefore she ran forth from house to house, making it known unto the people.

And they began to assemble themselves together unto the house of the king. And there came a multitude, and to their astonishment, they beheld the king, and the queen, and their servants prostrate upon the earth, and they all lay there as though they were dead; and they also saw Ammon, and behold, he was a Nephite. (Alma 19:1-18)

At this point, contention arose among the Lamanites as they observed the condition of their king and queen and their servants. Many thought "a great evil had come upon them." The story continues:

And thus the contention began to be exceeding sharp among them. And while they were thus contending, the woman servant who had caused the multitude to be gathered together came, and when she saw the contention which was among the multitude, she was exceeding sorrowful, even unto tears.

*And it came to pass that **she went and took the queen by the hand, that perhaps she might raise her from the ground; and as soon as she touched her hand, she arose and stood upon her feet**, and cried with a loud voice, saying: O blessed Jesus, who has saved me from an awful hell! O blessed God, have mercy on this people!*

*And when she had said this, she clasped her hands, being filled with joy, **speaking many words which were not understood; and when she had done this, she took the king, Lamoni, by the hand, and behold he arose and stood upon his feet.***

And it came to pass that when Ammon arose, he also administered unto them, and also did all the servants of Lamoni; and they did all declare unto the people the self-same thing—that their hearts had been changed; that they had no more desire to do evil.

And behold, many did declare unto the people that they had seen angels and had conversed with them; and thus they had told them things of God, and of his righteousness.

And it came to pass that there were many that did believe in their words; and as many as did believe were baptized; and they became a righteous people, and they did establish a church among them.

And thus the work of the Lord did commence among the Lamanites; thus the Lord did begin to pour out his Spirit upon them; and we see that his arm is extended to all people who will repent and believe on his name. (Alma 19:28-36)

Two courageous women played an integral part in this conversion story, as they were used by the Lord to accomplish His purposes.

Perhaps one of the most impressive stories of the Book of Mormon is also recorded by Alma, wherein he tells about the 2000 young Nephite warriors called "The Sons of Helaman", who "had been taught by their mothers":

> But behold, it came to pass they had many sons, who had not entered into a covenant that they would not take their weapons of war to defend themselves against their enemies; therefore they did assemble themselves together at this time, as many as were able to take up arms, and they called themselves Nephites.
>
> And they entered into a covenant to fight for the liberty of the Nephites, yea, to protect the land unto the laying down of their lives; yea, even they covenanted that they never would give up their liberty, but they would fight in all cases to protect the Nephites and themselves from bondage.
>
> Now behold, there were two thousand of those young men, who entered into this covenant and took their weapons of war to defend their country.
>
> And now behold, as they never had hitherto been a disadvantage to the Nephites, they became now at this period of time also a great support; for they took their weapons of war, and they would that Helaman should be their leader.
>
> And they were all young men, and they were exceedingly valiant for courage, and also for strength and activity; but behold, this was not all—they were men who were true at all times in whatsoever thing they were entrusted.
>
> Yea, they were men of truth and soberness, for they had been taught to keep the commandments of God and to walk uprightly before him. (Alma 53:16-21)

And Helaman goes on to describe the battle with the Lamanites:

> Therefore, what say ye, my sons, will ye go against them to battle?
>
> And now I say unto you, my beloved brother Moroni, that never had I seen so great courage, nay, not amongst all the Nephites. For as I had ever called them my sons (for they were all of them very young) even so they said unto me: Father, behold our God is

with us, and he will not suffer that we should fall; then let us go forth; we would not slay our brethren if they would let us alone; therefore let us go, lest they should overpower the army of Antipus.

*Now they never had fought, yet they did not fear death; and they did think more upon the liberty of their fathers than they did upon their lives; yea, **they had been taught by their mothers, that if they did not doubt, God would deliver them. And they rehearsed unto me the words of their mothers, saying: We do not doubt our mothers knew it.***

And it came to pass that I did return with my two thousand against these Lamanites who had pursued us. And now behold, the armies of Antipus had overtaken them, and a terrible battle had commenced.

The army of Antipus being weary, because of their long march in so short a space of time, were about to fall into the hands of the Lamanites; and had I not returned with my two thousand, they would have obtained their purpose. * * *

And now it came to pass that we, the people of Nephi, the people of Antipus, and I with my two thousand, did surround the Lamanites, and did slay them; yea, insomuch that they were compelled to deliver up their weapons of war and also themselves as prisoners of war.

And now it came to pass that when they had surrendered themselves up unto us, behold, I numbered those young men who had fought with me, fearing lest there were many of them slain.

*But behold, to my great joy, **there had not one soul of them fallen to the earth**; yea, and they had fought as if with the strength of God; yea, never were men known to have fought with such miraculous strength; and with such mighty power did they fall upon the Lamanites, that they did frighten them; and for this cause did the Lamanites deliver themselves up as prisoners of war. (Alma 56:44-50; 54-56)*

Evidently, the mothers of these 2,000 young warriors had taught them well the things of God, and had set righteous examples for them to follow. What a tribute to these mothers who had such an influence upon their sons! They were indeed a great credit to their husbands and to their God!

Other recorded incidents illustrate the sufferings, faith and joy of Nephite and Lamanite women. Many of them witnessed the appearance of the Savior after His crucifixion, as recorded in Third Nephi. The people had just experienced a terrible destruction in the land, and a multitude of the survivors gathered "round about the temple which was in the land Bountiful". A voice from heaven declared:

Behold my Beloved Son, in whom I am well pleased, in whom I have glorified my name—hear ye him.

And it came to pass, as they understood, they cast their eyes up again towards heaven; and behold, they saw a Man descending out of heaven; and he was clothed in a white robe; and he came down and stood in the midst of them; and the eyes of the whole multitude were turned upon him, and they durst not open their mouths, even one to another, and wist not what it meant, for they thought it was an angel that had appeared unto them.

*And it came to pass that he stretched forth his hand and spake unto the people, saying: Behold, I am Jesus Christ, whom the prophets testified shall come into the world. * * ***

And it came to pass that when Jesus had spoken these words the whole multitude fell to the earth; for they remembered that it had been prophesied among them that Christ should show himself unto them [men and women] after his ascension into heaven.

And it came to pass that the Lord spake unto them saying: Arise and come forth unto me, that ye may thrust your hands into my side, and also that ye may feel the prints of the nails in my hands and in my feet, that ye may know that I am the God of Israel, and the God of the whole earth, and have been slain for the sins of the world.

And it came to pass that the multitude went forth, and thrust their hands into his side, and did feel the prints of the nails in his hands and in his feet; and this they did do, going forth one by one until they had all gone forth, and did see with their eyes and did feel with their hands, and did know of a surety and did bear record, that it was he, of whom it was written by the prophets, that should come.

And when they had all gone forth and had witnessed for themselves, they did cry out with one accord, saying: Hosanna! Blessed be the name of the Most High God! And they did fall down at the feet of Jesus, and did worship him. (3 Nephi 11:8-10, 12-17)

The Savior taught the people for a considerable time, and then said to them:

I see that your faith is sufficient that I should heal you.

And it came to pass that when he had thus spoken, all the multitude, with one accord, did go forth with their sick and their afflicted, and their lame, and with their blind, and with their dumb, and with all them that were afflicted in any manner; and he did heal them every one as they were brought forth unto him.

And they did all, both they who had been healed and they who were whole, bow down at his feet, and did worship him; and as many as could come for the multitude did kiss his feet, insomuch that they did bathe his feet with their tears.

And it came to pass that he commanded that their little children should be brought. So they brought their little children and set them down upon the ground round about him, and Jesus stood in the midst; and the multitude gave way till they had all been brought unto him. (3 Nephi 17:8-12)

And after this manner do they bear record: The eye hath never seen, neither hath the ear heard, before, so great and marvelous things as we saw and heard Jesus speak unto the Father;

And no tongue can speak, neither can there be written by any man, neither can the hearts of men conceive so great and marvelous things as we both saw and heard Jesus speak; and no one can conceive of the joy which filled our souls at the time we heard him pray for us unto the Father. (3 Nephi 17:16-17)

And as they looked to behold they cast their eyes towards heaven, and they saw the heavens open, and they saw angels descending out of heaven as it were in the midst of fire; and they came down and encircled those little ones about, and they were encircled about with fire; and the angels did minister unto them.

And the multitude did see and hear and bear record; and they know that their record is true for they all of them did see and hear, every man for himself; and they were in number about two thousand and five hundred souls; and they did consist of men, women, and children. (3 Nephi 17:24-25)

It should be remembered that even though scriptural accounts usually refer to just the men, oftentimes women were present as well, and they, too, experienced these spiritual outpourings. And sometimes they went to battle and were killed along with their husbands:

And it came to pass when Coriantumr had recovered of his wounds, he began to remember the words which Ether had spoken unto him.

*He saw that there had been slain by the sword already nearly **two millions of his people**, and he began to sorrow in his heart; yea, there had been slain two millions of mighty men, and also their **wives and their children**. * * ***

Wherefore, they were for the space of four years gathering together the people, that they might get all who were upon the face of the land, and that they might receive all the strength which it was possible that they could receive.

*And it came to pass that when they were all gathered together, every one to the army which he would, **with their wives and their children—***

both men, women and children being armed with weapons of war, having shields, and breast-plates, and head-plates, and being clothed after the manner of war—they did march forth one against another to battle; and they fought all that day, and conquered not. (Ether 15:1-2, 14-15)

And the women also suffered as prisoners of war and were offered as sacrifices. According to Mormon:

And it is impossible for the tongue to describe, or for man to write a perfect description of the horrible scene of the blood and carnage which was among the people, both of the Nephites and of the Lamanites; and every heart was hardened, so that they delighted in the shedding of blood continually. And there never had been so great wickedness among all the children of Lehi, nor even among all the house of Israel, according to the words of the Lord, as was among this people.

And it came to pass that the Lamanites did take possession of the city Desolation, and this because their number did exceed the number of the Nephites.

And they did also march forward against the city Teancum, and did drive the inhabitants forth out of her, and did take many prisoners both women and children, and did offer them up as sacrifices unto their idol gods.

And it came to pass that in the three hundred and sixty and seventh year, the Nephites being angry because the Lamanites had sacrificed their women and their children, that they did go against the Lamanites with exceeding great anger, insomuch that they did beat again the Lamanites, and drive them out of their lands. (Mormon 4:11-15)

And in the final battles that followed, women and children were slain right along with the men; "and their flesh, and bones, and blood lay upon the face of the earth, . . ." (Mormon 6:15)

Thus we see that in the Book of Mormon men became prophets and women prophetesses; men went to battle as warriors and were injured or killed—and so did the women. The sisters shared spiritual manifestations right along with their husbands, including the blessings and powers of the Priesthood.

* * *

Just as someone enjoying the gifts of the spirit will not necessarily be blessed with the exercise of **all** the spiritual gifts, so it is with those who have Priesthood—they do not hold **all** of the offices in that Priesthood. Whatever relationship women may have to Priesthood, it is evident that they are not to be called to function in church Priesthood offices. But a righteous woman cannot be deprived of the **blessings, powers, and privileges** of the Priesthood. This will be discussed in more detail in a later chapter.

Chapter 4

PROPER ORDER

IN THE PRIESTHOOD

Women's relationship to the Priesthood has been a controversial issue in the Church for decades. The generally accepted, but very restrictive, position today is illustrated in the following story told by Leah Widtsoe about a conversation between a small boy and his sister:

*The boy stated he could be an engineer when he grew up and drive a huge engine. The girl said she could be a great musician and thrill great audiences with the joy of her art. The boy retorted that he could be President of the United States. For a while the little girl was somewhat silenced for surely here her brother had the better of the argument. Suddenly a bright thought came. "When I grow up, I can be a mother and have a baby all my own and nurse it!" That seemed to silence the lad until this bright thought came, "But I can hold the Priesthood!" ("Priesthood and Womanhood," **Relief Society Mag.**, Oct. 1933, p. 598)*

This young boy, like most Elders in the Church, had acquired a narrow view of the relationship of women to the Priesthood.

The Apostle Paul gave a more liberal interpretation—"Nevertheless neither is the man without the woman, neither the woman without the man, in the Lord." (I Cor. 11:11) He took the position that both men and women share in the divine blessings of the Priesthood.

Priesthood Definition

Before proceeding any further, let us review some definitions of Priesthood:

Brigham Young: "an invisible, almighty, **God-like power**" (JD 3:259); "a perfect **order and system** of **government.**" (JD 13:242); "perfect order, laws, rules regulations, organization; it forms, fashions, makes, creates, produces, protects and holds in existence the inhabitants of the earth in a pure and holy form of government, preparatory to entering the kingdom of Heaven." (JD 13:281)

John Taylor: "It is the **rule and government of God,** whether on earth, or in the heavens; and it is the only legitimate power, the only authority that is acknowledged by Him to **rule and regulate the affairs of His kingdom**. When every wrong thing shall be put right, and all usurpers shall be put down, when he whose right it is to reign shall take the dominion, then nothing but the Priesthood will bear rule; it alone will sway the sceptre of authority in heaven and on earth, for this is the legitimacy of God." (JD 1:224)

Wilford Woodruff: "It is the authority of God in heaven to the sons of men **to administer in any of the ordinances** of His house." (JD 16:266)

Bruce R. McConkie: "Priesthood is the **power and authority of God** delegated to man on earth to act in all things for the salvation of men." **(Morm. Doc.**, 1958, p. 534)

Rodney Turner: "Priesthood is the **authority and power** to organize sustain, direct, redeem and sanctify." **(Woman and the Priesthood**, p. 302)

A more detailed description comes from the **Millennial Star:**

> *All power is not immediately derived from the same source, but all legitimate* **right of Government** *is in the Priesthood of God. * * **
>
> *By this we learn that the Priesthood administers in a perfect organization or government, because it is the* **government** *ordained, upheld, by a perfect Being. It is a holy and just* **authority**, *because it administers in things pertaining to God, and partakes of the virtue of all His attributes. It is reasonable, then, for us to conclude that God would require obedience and respect to be paid to His government wherever found, and that those who hold the Priesthood should be recognized as His messengers. (Priesthood editorial,* **Mill. Star** *14:593)*

With the use of such terms as "rule", "power", "government", and "authority," these definitions seem to be describing a **patriarchal** rather than matriarchal organization. Heber C. Kimball explained:

> **Women were never placed to lead**. *Did you ever see a ship rigged for sailing to England, or to any other port in the world, without a helm, and rudder, and a man who knew the points of the compass and how to receive instructions for guiding that ship. And then you will sometimes see a number of boats lashed with cables to a large ship, and they are all led by that ship, and that is guided by the power and intelligence on board of it.* **Women are made to be led**, *and counselled, and directed. If they are not led, and do not make their cables fast to the power and authority they are connected with, they will be damned. Instead of cutting those little fibres that pertain to those cables which connect them with the ship, they ought to be adding other strands to the cables, that they may stand when the sea becomes boisterous. * * **

Women are to be led. If I should undertake to drive a woman, I should have to drive her before me; and then she becomes my leader the moment I do that. I should lead her; and she should be led by me, if I am a good man; and if I am not a good man, I have no just right in this Church to a wife or wives, or to the power to propagate my species. What, then, should be done with me? Make a eunuch of me, and stop my propagation. (JD 5:29)

Brigham Young also understood and tried to convey this correct order of Priesthood to the Saints:

*Sisters have no right to **meddle in the affairs of the Kingdom of God**. They never can hold the Priesthood apart from their husbands. (**Seventies Record**, March 9, 1845)*

The Prophet Isaiah warned about women who rule:

*As for **my people**, children are their oppressors, and women rule over them. O my people, they which lead thee cause thee to err, and destroy the way of they paths. (Isa.3:12)*

However, this does not mean that men, as Priesthood holders, should not give the proper respect and consideration to women:

*The possession of the Priesthood and its consequent family leadership should make men very considerate of women. The man who arrogantly feels that he is better than his wife because he holds the Priesthood, has failed utterly to comprehend the meaning and purpose of Priesthood. He needs to remember that the Lord loves His daughters quite as well as His sons. It is but a small and puny-souled man who could wish to humiliate women as a class and keep them as an inferior sex; for men can never rise superior to the women who bear and nurture them. (**Priesthd. and Chur. Gover**., John A. Widtsoe, p. 89)*

Through the years, however, the definition of the word **Priesthood** has changed. Linda K. Newell noted this in her article "The Historical Relationship of Mormon Women and Priesthood":

> *Thus Priesthood was defined not only as power from God but also as* **the man upon whom it was conferred.** *Statements such as this initiated the practice of referring to leaders and eventually to all male members as "the priesthood." Joseph Fielding Smith, a young apostle in 1910, put the case even stronger in a conference talk on respecting the presiding brethren, particularly the first Presidency: "It is a serious thing for any member of this Church to raise his voice against the priesthood, or to hold the priesthood in disrespect; for the Lord will not hold such guiltless." (***Conf. Rept***. Oct. 1910, p. 39)*

It is interesting to note the evolution and changes in both terminology and doctrines in the 160+ years of LDS Church history. Undoubtedly with Linda Newell's above concept in mind, Margaret Toscano also commented:

> *Instead of being an instrument for spiritual empowerment to lead each individual to God, the priesthood is too often used to compel obedience to an earthly power system which privileges some people above others. I believe that the* **priesthood has become the chief idol of the modern church because it is the object we are asked to give allegiance to, above Christ himself.** *("If Mormon Women Have Had the Priesthood Since 1843, Why Aren't They Using It?"* **Dialogue** *27:2, Summer 1994, p. 226)*

The Nature of Women

It is an historical fact that women are not actually the weaker sex, but in many instances have fared better physically than men. The trek from Illinois to the Salt Lake Valley was proof of that. Even in spiritual things she is often superior, as Brigham Young said on several occasions:

> *Women are more ready to do and love the right than men are; and if they could have a little guidance, and were encouraged to carry out the instincts of their nature, they would effect a revolution for good in any community a great deal quicker than men can accomplish it. (JD 12:194)*

> *The men are the lords of the earth, and they are more inclined to reject the Gospel than the women. The women are a great deal more inclined to believe the truth than the men; they comprehend it more quickly, and they are submissive and easy to teach. . . . (JD 14:120)*

> *. . . he is by nature coarser and more prone to such wickedness than she is. Woman is altogether of a finer nature, and has stronger moral inclinations; it is not natural for her to indulge in wickedness that man takes common delight in. (JD 18:233)*

John Taylor also described the nature and proper treatment of women:

> *Should we not protect them? Do we profess to be in the image of God, holding the holy priesthood of God, and then would we treat the fair daughters of Zion with contempt, or permit them to be injured or imposed upon in any way? God forbid. They are flesh of our flesh, bone of our bone; they are our helpmeets, and our associations and our relations with them ought to be pleasant and agreeable and with all long suffering and fidelity. (JD 20:178)*

In this world of apparent male domination in both spiritual and temporal arenas, men, in general, have momentarily forgotten the rightful position of women. Either because of ignorance or neglect, men have committed a serious oversight, resulting in major problems. As Dr. Rodney Turner expressed:

. . . it is safe to say that, with but a very few exceptions, women have never been shown the respect, protection, guidance or love they both needed and deserved. They are the betrayed sex. Unfortunately many modern women are compounding their plight by betraying themselves in new and more damaging ways. Still, the cause of womankind is just. If they are to plead it effectively, they must understand what their true cause is, what God willed for them in the beginning, and why he said, "thy desire shall be to thy husband, and he shall rule over thee." (**Women and the Priesthood**, p. 45)

The great catastrophe of our age is the active participation of women in Babylon in their efforts to gain "proper" respect and individual rights. They have sought recognition in the fashions of Paris, the artistry of Rome, the makeup styles of New York and Hollywood, and the political directives of Washington, D.C. These should not be the sources of inspirational guidance for modern-day Israel. There are even passages of scripture warning us against these trends. Consider this descriptive passage from Isaiah:

Moreover the Lord saith, because the **daughters of Zion** *are haughty, and walk with stretched forth necks and wanton eyes, walking and mincing as they go, and making a tinkling with their feet: Therefore the Lord will smite with a scab the crown of the head of the daughters of Zion, and the Lord will discover their secret parts.*

In that day the Lord will take away the bravery of their tinkling ornaments about their feet, and their cauls, and their round tires like the moon, the chains, and the bracelets, and the mufflers, the bonnets, and the ornaments of the legs, and the headbands, and the tablets, and the earrings, the rings, and nose jewels, the changeable suits of apparel, and the mantles, and the wimples, and the crisping pins, the glasses, and the fine linen, and the hoods, and the vails.

> *And it shall come to pass, that instead of sweet smell there shall be stink; and instead of a girdle a rent; and instead of well set hair baldness; and instead of a stomacher a girding of sackcloth; and burning instead of beauty. (Isa. 3:16-24)*

Many present-day women's movements are promoting competition with men, seeking greater wealth and higher position, and supporting the attainment of a better social and political status—instead of encouraging a more valiant fulfillment of their role at home with their family. Today's women frequently reject or neglect children. But none of this really frees women, but rather enslaves them in the financial and political world of mammon.

With an increase in woman's responsibility, position and authority, come added penalties should she be guilty of disobedience. If women were to hold the Priesthood, they would be in serious jeopardy if they did not honor it:

> *There are thousands of men and women among the nations of the earth that it will be more tolerable for, in the day of judgment, than it will for you, if you violate your calling and* ***do not honour your priesthood***. *You know that it was declared that it would be more tolerable for Sodom and Gomorrah than for the children of God who had received the priesthood, and heard the voice of a prophet, and disobeyed it. (Heber C. Kimball, JD 5:30)*

Could it be that God in His mercy, and because of His great love and respect for womanhood, is protecting women from the possibility of coming under such a curse?

In order to maintain the proper perspective, maybe we should keep in mind the source from which women come:

*Now, from whence did you come, sisters? From whence spring you and your children? You spring from these main limbs and **from that Priesthood**. If you did not spring out of the Priesthood, where did you come from? Not many of you have legally sprung out of the Priesthood anywhere in the world in the latter days; but if you have a legal man, **who has a legal Priesthood**, you can raise heirs to the kingdom of God, and they become connected with it, without any of your washings, anointings, and sealings. (Heber C. Kimball, JD 5:31)*

Keys and Dominion

In previous dispensations when the Gospel was on the earth, the **keys** of the Priesthood have always been held by men, as Joseph Smith explained:

*Paul spoke of the dispensation of the fullness of times, when God would gather together all things in one, etc.; and those **men** to whom these **keys** have been given, will have to be there. . . . (TPJS, p. 159)*

And with the gospel restoration in our dispensation it was no different; Joseph Smith held those keys and always will:

*. . . I went into the woods to inquire of the Lord, by prayer, His will concerning me, and I saw an angel, and he laid his hands upon my head, and ordained me to a Priest after the order of Aaron, and to hold the **keys of this Priesthood**, . . . (TPJS, p. 335)*

But the Priesthood itself is for the guidance of all righteous men:

*A **man** can do nothing for himself unless God direct him in the right way; and the **Priesthood is for that purpose**. (TPJS, p. 364)*

As it was in the days of Christ, so it was in the latter days: Christ selected 12 **men** to whom He gave the authority of Priesthood to establish His ministry. The Prophet Joseph was also commanded to establish a quorum of 12 **men** to do the same in this dispensation.

Why have men had so much dominion in the Priesthood?

1. Nearly all ancient prophets were men.
2. The Book of Mormon records no prophetic women.
3. Christ chose men for the work of His ministry.
4. Men have had the responsibility to record and trans late ancient records and scripture.
5. Men are predominantly the recipients of written revelations.
6. Priesthood callings and proselyting missions have been directed mainly to men.
7. Priesthood lineage is traced through the direct line of men.
8. The nature and order of Priesthood is patriarchal rather than matriarchal.
9. When the Aaronic Priesthood was restored, it came by way of a man who gave it to two other men. Likewise, the Melchizedek Priesthood came through three men who conferred it on two other men.
10. When certain keys and callings were given by mani festation in the Kirtland Temple, there were at least four heavenly beings who made an appearance in that temple—all of them men.
11. When the Father and/or the Son have had special messages to deliver on earth, they have seldom come to or from a woman.
12. The greatest manifestations have been of the Father and the Son, but not the Mother.

And the list could go on and on. One of the orders of Priesthood rule is that men preside, as Dr. Turner states:

> *The voice of the priesthood is a male voice; nowhere in all scripture is there record of any female being heard speaking in behalf of God. The Lord does not send women to do the work of men; it is not for women to receive instructions for the Church and kingdom and priesthood of God. The message of salvation is a priesthood message delivered by male messengers to male prophets. It is all under the direction of the Godhead— three male deities. (**Women and the Priesthood**, p. 285)*

Professor Turner goes on to mention the consequences for disobeying these instructions:

> *Each has proper labors to perform and a proper place in which to perform them. If women do the work of men and men do the work of women, the result is confusion, strife, insecurity and a loss of basic identities. (**Ibid.**, p. 285)*

Yet most of God's revelations pertain to both men and women, with some to men alone and others directed only to women. Misunderstandings that arise are because men and women do not comprehend their respective roles, callings and responsibilities.

An excellent example of dominion in the relationship of men and women and also pertaining to the Kingdom of God and the Church is given to us by John the Revelator:

> *And there appeared a great sign in heaven, in the likeness of things on the earth; a **woman** clothed with the sun, and the moon under her feet, and upon her head a crown of twelve stars.*
> *And the woman being with child, cried, travailing in birth, and pained to be delivered. And **she brought**

forth a man child, who was to rule all nations with a rod of iron; and her child was caught up unto God and his throne.

And there appeared another sign in heaven; and behold, a great red dragon, having seven heads and ten horns, and seven crowns upon his heads. ***

And the dragon prevailed not against Michael, neither the child, nor the **woman which was the church of God***, who had been delivered of her pains, and* **brought forth the kingdom of our God** *and his Christ. (Revel. 12:1-4, 7)*

Note the following salient points in this analogy:

1. The woman was the Church of God.
2. She brought forth a man child who was to rule all nations.
3. She brought forth the Kingdom of God.

It is significant that the woman, or Church, gives birth to the man, or Kingdom of God, who then rules and has dominion over all—including the woman and the Church. Even though men are born from women, they ultimately have the right to rule (in righteousness), with the woman living within man's protection, authority and dominion. Likewise the Church will be in subjection to and under the dominion of the Kingdom of God.

Roles of Men and Women

False prophets and worldly leaders in the political, social, educational and religious realms have been tearing down the traditional roles of both wife and mother and the family patriarch. Women are being used falsely without their being aware of it. Modern-day pressures are telling her to be "free"—even at the cost of all else.

Naturally a husband who does not honor Christ as his Head does not receive proper respect from a righteous wife. No one owes allegiance to those who are out of harmony with God. Children often fail if they have a wayward mother; a wife will usually shun and reject a wicked husband; and men will try to retreat from a corrupt church or government that has become a law to itself. Brigham Young's advice was:

> It is not my general practice to counsel the sisters to disobey their husbands, but my counsel is—obey your husbands; and I am sanguine and most emphatic on that subject. But I never counselled a woman to follow her husband to the devil. If a man is determined to expose the lives of his friends, let that man go to the devil and to destruction alone. (JD 1:77)
>
> If the men of the world would be honest and full of good works, you would not see them living as they do. And the women are entitled to the kingdom, they are entitled to the glory, they are entitled to exaltation if they are obedient to the Priesthood, and they will be crowned with those that are crowned. (JD 16:167)

But a woman still has her free agency in these matters:

> But has not a woman the same volition that the man has? Can she not follow or disobey the man as he can follow or disobey Christ? Certainly she can; she is responsible for her acts, and must answer for them. She is endowed with intelligence and judgment, and will stand upon her own merits as much so as the man. ***
>
> The man is responsible for the woman only so far as she is influenced by, or is obedient to, his counsels. Christ is responsible for the man so far as the man walks in obedience to the laws and commandments he has given, but no further, and so far will his atoning blood redeem and cleanse from sin; so far as they obey them will the principles of eternal life revealed in the Gospel have effect upon the souls of men, so also with women. So, sisters, do not flatter yourselves that you

have nothing to answer for so long as you may have a good husband. You must be obedient. (Joseph F. Smith, JD 16:247)

Elder H. W. Naisbitt declared:

The best conditions are where there is a devoted man and a devoted woman, or women, all laboring in the interests of the Kingdom of God upon the earth, and impressing their own individuality, by the powers of an educational character upon the posterity that God may give them. (JD 26:120)

Women should recognize that men and women are equal in many ways and yet they are physically different and their qualifications and stewardships are different. And they are certainly not meant to be the same. As the expression goes, "Dogs don't climb trees, and cats don't swim."

Much of what are called civil liberties, equality, rights and privileges tend to lead men and women away from those opportunities and rights that God has already given them. Social and political leaders are putting words into God's mouth and interpreting His commands to accommodate their own will.

Jesus said, "I do always those things that please Him." (John 8:29) Today the cry is to do anything to please ourselves, taking the attitude that "not thy will, but mine be done." All of these things have led women away from the Priesthood rather than toward it.

The Prophet Joseph Smith made the following promises to worthy women of the Relief Society:

At two o'clock I met the members of the "Female Relief Society," and after presiding at the admission of many new members, gave a lecture on the Priesthood,

*showing how **the sisters would come in possession
of the privileges, blessings and gifts of the
Priesthood**, and that the signs should follow them, such
as healing the sick, casting out devils, etc., and that they
might attain unto these blessings by a virtuous life, and
conversation, and diligence in keeping all the commandments; a synopsis of which was reported by Miss Eliza
R. Snow. (DHC 4:602)*

With such promises awaiting them, it is difficult to
understand why women in the Church would trade these
blessings for a mess of pottage. Hugh Nibley observed:

*Nothing pleases God more than to have his children
"seek greater light and knowledge"—it was for that that
Adam, Abraham, Enoch, Moses, and Joseph Smith were
rewarded with the richest blessings. Nothing displeases
him more than to have them "seek for power, and
authority, and riches" (3 Nephi 6:15). Through the years
the Latter-day Saints have consistently sought not for
the former but for the latter. It is only right and proper
that we should stew in our own juice for a while.
("Priesthood", Hugh Nibley, **Sunstone** 14:6, Dec. 1990,
p. 11)*

Conferral of Priesthood

Throughout Church history the importance of correct
Priesthood conferral has been stressed over and over
again—even to the point that if it is not done correctly,
the man's Priesthood authority is in jeopardy. For conferring both the Aaronic and Melchizedek Priesthoods,
the correct patterns have been given:

*(John the Baptist to Joseph Smith and Oliver
Cowdery—) "Upon you my fellow servants, in the name
of Messiah, **I confer the Priesthood of Aaron**, which
holds the keys of the ministering of angels, and of the
gospel of repentance, and of baptism by immersion for*

the remission of sins: and this shall never be taken again from the earth until the sons of Levi do offer again an offering unto the Lord in righteousness." (P of GP, Jos. Smith 2:69)

*(After calling the person by name the officiating Elder should say:) "In the name of Jesus Christ, and by the authority of the Melchizedek Priesthood vested in us, we lay our hands upon your head and **confer upon you the Melchizedek Priesthood**, and ordain you to the office of an elder in the Church of Jesus Christ of Latter-day Saints." etc. (**The Elders Manual**, p. 51, April 1, 1914, Joseph F. Smith, President)*

Included below are just a few of the many references on the importance of proper Priesthood conferral: (For more information, see **The Holy Priesthood,** Vol. 1, "Conferral and Ordinations of the Priesthood," Kraut)

*For every high priest taken from among men is ordained for men in things pertaining to God, that he may offer both gifts and sacrifices for sins: * * * And no man taketh this honour unto himself, but **he that is called of God, as was Aaron**. (Heb. 5:1, 4)*

*We are obliged to confer upon them the Melchizedek Priesthood. . . . (Brigham Young, **Disc. of B.Y.**, p. 396)*

*Most of you, my brethren, are Elders, Seventies, or High Priests; perhaps there is not a Priest or Teacher present. The reason of this is that when we give the brethren their endowments, we are obliged to **confer** upon them the Melchizedek Priesthood (**before** they get their endowments). (Brigham Young, JD 18:309)*

*He said his name was John, the same who came to prepare the way of our Savior at His first coming, and that he was sent to **confer this lesser Priest-***

hood *upon His servants in answer to their prayers. . . .*
(Orson Pratt, JD 12:360)

. . . the Priesthood which I [the Lord] have **conferred**
upon the seed of Levi, shall remain just as **eternal** *as*
the new heavens and the new earth. (Orson Pratt, JD
12:361)

We may notice that John the Baptist **conferred the**
Priesthood *upon Joseph Smith, and that therefore, as*
he held it, he had the power to **confer it upon others.**
(John Taylor, **Gospel Kingdom,** *p. 156)*

There is only one way to confer Priesthood, and that is
to confer it. (Truth *9:117)*

Through the laying on of hands *the Priesthood is*
conferred upon those who are counted worthy to receive
it. (Erastus Snow, JD 25:199)

The Lord has given unto us the Priesthood. This is
conferred upon us *that we may administer in the ordi-*
nances of life and salvation. (Wilford Woodruff, JD
23:328)

I [Abraham Cannon] maintained that it was necessary
to say in the ordination that **this [the Melchizedek**
Priesthood] was conferred upon him; otherwise he
did not possess it. *(Abraham H. Cannon Journal,*
March 20, 1887)

The person ordained should have the Aaronic
Priesthood conferred upon him in connection with his
ordination. **He cannot receive a portion or fragment**
of the Aaronic Priesthood, *because that would be act-*
ing on the idea that either or both of the Priesthoods
were subject to subdivision, which is contrary to revela-
tion. (Joseph F. Smith, **Imp. Era** *4:394, March 1901)*

Whenever the Priesthood is delegated to man, it is
conferred *upon him, . . . (David O. McKay,* **Era,** *June*
1959, p. 406)

On more than one occasion, John Taylor—who "set apart" the first Relief Society Presidency—admitted that he conferred NO PRIESTHOOD on these sisters:

> I [John Taylor] was in Nauvoo at the time the Relief Society was organized by the Prophet Joseph Smith, and I was present on the occasion. At a late meeting of the Society held in Salt Lake City I was present, and I read from a record called the Book of the Law of the Lord, the minutes of that meeting. At that meeting the Prophet called Sister Emma to be an elect lady. That means that she was called to a certain work; and that was in fulfillment of a certain revelation concerning her. She was elected to preside over the Relief Society, and she was ordained to expound the Scriptures. In compliance with Brother Joseph's request, I set her apart, and also ordained Sister Whitney, wife of Bishop Newel K. Whitney, and Sister Cleveland, wife of Judge Cleveland, to be her counselors. Some of the sisters have thought that these sisters mentioned were, in this ordination, **ordained to the priesthood.** And for the information of all interested in this subject I will say it is **not the calling of these sisters to hold the Priesthood,** only in connection with their husbands, . . . (JD 21:367-68)
>
> Because Emma had already been "ordain'd [set apart] at the time the Revelation was given," she was not set apart at this time with her counselors. Rather, John Taylor "confirm'd upon her all the blessings which had been confer'd on her, . . ." (**Nauvoo Minutes**, Mar. 17, 1842) (Note: The distinction between "ordain," as the conferral of Priesthood, and "set apart," as the delegation of authority in the Church, would not be made until the Utah period, sometime before 1880. — **Women of Covenant**, ftnt. 21, p. 444)
>
> Elder Taylor also blessed the two counselors, Sarah M. Cleveland and Elizabeth Ann Whitney, in connection with their ordination. He later explained that theirs was **not an ordination to the priesthood,** but rather a blessing that set them apart for

*their new positions. (**Woman's Exponent** 9:53-54, Sept. 1, 1880, as quoted in **Women of Covenant: The Story of Relief Society**, Derr, Cannon, and Beecher, p. 29)*

And, referring to the LDS sisters in general, this same position was reiterated nearly 80 years later:

*While the sisters have not been given the Priesthood, **it has not been conferred upon them**, that does not mean the Lord has not given unto them authority. Authority and priesthood are two different things. (Joseph Fielding Smith, "Relief Society—An Aid to the Priesthood," **R.S. Mag.** 46:4, Jan. 1959)*

After analyzing the information in this "Conferral of Priesthood" section, the following questions should be considered:

1. If it is so important for men to have Priesthood **conferred** correctly, why would it not be just as important for women to have such a conferral? (There is no place in scripture or Church history where instructions are given for women to have the Priesthood conferred upon them.)

2. If a woman does indeed have the Melchizedek Priesthood, she should have, according to John Taylor, "the power to confer it upon others." When and where has such an event transpired?

3. Why is it that men have to have the Melchizedek Priesthood conferred upon them **before** they get their endowments, and yet women would be favored to get it **during** their endowments?

4. If any sisters in the gospel were deserving and in need
   of holding the Priesthood, it certainly should have
   been the first Relief Society presidency; and yet, John
   Taylor admitted that when he "set them apart" he did
   not confer any Priesthood.

Patriarchal Order

As previously mentioned, the Holy Priesthood is patriarchal rather than matriarchal, and rightly so. The
Prophet Joseph explained that "there are three grand
orders of priesthood," one of which is Patriarchal (TPJS,
p. 322). Hyrum Smith and his father were among those
who have held the keys of this Priesthood authority.
(Ibid., see p. 40) A Patriarch is also called an Evangelist,
as Joseph Smith explained:

> An Evangelist is a Patriarch, even the oldest man of
> the blood of Joseph or of the seed of Abraham. Wherever
> the Church of Christ is established in the earth, there
> should be a Patriarch for the benefit of the posterity of
> the Saints, as it was with Jacob in giving his patriarchal
> blessing unto his sons, etc. [June 27, 1839] (DHC 3:381)

The Prophet also stated that by going to the temple
"you will then receive more knowledge concerning this
priesthood," (TPJS, p. 322), and that "all priesthood is
Melchizedek, but there are different portions or degrees
of it." (TPJS, p. 180)

(More information on these three grand orders of
Priesthood will follow in a future volume of The **Holy
Priesthood** series.)

There is a patriarchal or fatherly type of order to
Priesthood authority, rather than a military or dictatorial authority. When Adam was given the right to "rule
over" his wife, it did not give him dictatorial power. The
man has the rights of presidency, which is responsibility.

No power or influence can or ought to be maintained by virtue of the priesthood, only by persuasion, by long-suffering, by gentleness and meekness, and by love unfeigned; by kindness, and pure knowledge, which shall greatly enlarge the soul without hypocrisy, and without guile. (D & C 121:41-42)

Through such conduct, the husband will **deserve** the love and respect of his wife. It is obvious that the wife is to obey the laws of her husband only as he obeys the laws of God.

A woman does not act in the office or calling of a Priesthood quorum, but she does share in all of its rights, powers, privileges, and blessings. There is not much significant difference. As David Rockefeller once said, "If I own a company, or manage it, does it make any difference?"

The Priesthood might be compared to an umbrella held by the righteous husband, or Patriarch of the family. His wife (or wives) may stand under that umbrella with him and enjoy the same shelter and protection from rain, snow, or sun. But it is the Patriarch's role and responsibility to **hold** the umbrella for his family while they all receive and enjoy the same blessings.

To be the patriarch of a family or to share in the same rights and blessings as the patriarch is not much different. This was explained by the Lord to Emma Smith:

Let thy soul delight in thy husband, and the glory which shall come upon him. Keep my commandments continually, and a crown of righteousness thou shalt receive. And except thou do this, where I am you cannot come. (D & C 25:14-15)

This correct order is carried out with men as well as it is for women. Every man holding Priesthood is also under this patriarchal order and a duty to that subjection, as explained:

I have counseled every woman of this church to let her husband be her file leader; he leads her and those above him in the Priesthood lead him. But I never counseled a woman to follow her husband to hell." (Brigham Young, as quoted in R.S. Magazine, Nov. 1933, p. 669)

There will never be any such thing there as being from under their father's rule, no matter whether twenty-one or twenty-one thousand years of age, it will make no difference, they will still be subject to the laws of their Patriarch or Father, and they must observe and obey them throughout all eternity. (Orson Pratt, JD 15:320)

Matriarchal Responsibilities

The Priesthood in a marriage should involve the sharing of both responsibilities and blessings. The man has his own duties just as the women has hers. In a family, a business, a church or a government, their members have different functions, but they are cooperative. Brigham Young clearly explained the order and duties of women in relation to the Priesthood in the family:

*It depends in a great degree upon the mother, as to what children receive, in early age, of principle of every description, pertaining to all that can be learned by the human family. . . . I can see mothers pay attention to everything under heaven, but the training up of their children in the way they should go, and they will even make it appear obligatory on the father to take care of the child at a year old. . . . I will tell you the truth as you will find it in eternity. If your children do not receive impressions of true piety, virtue, tenderness, and every principle of the holy Gospel, **you may be assured that their sins will not be required at the hands of the father, but of the mother**. Lay it to heart, ye mothers, for it will unavoidably be so. The duty of the mother is to watch* *over his children, and give them their early education, for impressions received in infancy are lasting. You know, yourselves, by experience, that the impressions you have received in the dawn of your mortal existence, bear, to this day, with the greatest weight upon your mind. It is the experience of people generally, that what they imbibe from their mothers in infancy, is the most lasting upon the mind through life. This is natural, it is reasonable, it is right. I do not suppose you can find one person among five hundred, who does not think his mother to be the best woman that ever lived. This is right, it is planted in the human heart. The child reposes implicit confidence in the mother, you behold in him a natural attachment, no matter what her appearance may be, that makes him think his mother is the best and handsomest mother in the world. I speak for myself. Children have all confidence in their mothers; and if mothers would take proper pains, they can instil into the hearts of their children what they please. You will, no doubt, recollect reading, in the Book of Mormon, of two thousand young men, who were brought up to believe that, if they put their whole trust in God, and served Him, no power would overcome them. You also recollect reading of them going out to fight, and so bold were they, and so mighty their faith, that it was impossible for their enemies to slay them. This power and faith they obtained through the teachings of their mothers. The character of a person is formed through life, to a greater or less degree, by the teachings of the mother. The traits of early impressions that she gives the child, will be characteristic points in his character through every avenue of his mortal existence. (B.Y., JD 1:66-67)*

When God created male and female, He gave instructions as to their duties—to the woman He said, "In sorrow thou shalt bring forth children"; and to the man, "By the sweat of thy face shalt thou eat bread." Each was to be responsible for his or her own special areas. Dr. Rodney Turned stated:

*Not only should men and women manifest their shared human traits and emotions within their respective natures, it is also imperative that they honor those roles which are indigenous to those natures. Men must act the part of men—beings sons, husbands, fathers, providers, agents of God in the world at large, and brothers to their brothers. Women must act the part of women—being daughters, wives, mothers, homemakers, teachers and guides of their children and sisters to their sisters. These are the core roles each is ordained to play. All other things are secondary to them. When men and women cannot or will not fulfill these roles, society is thrown off balance with resulting disorder and suffering. (**Woman and the Priesthood**, p. 18)*

Regarding these roles and responsibilities, this last dispensation has provided more light and knowledge for us than probably any other. However, on the other hand, there is also more temptation, misinformation, and apostasy creating confusion and disorder—especially for women who are trying to find their correct place in the community and in their families. This is the subject of our next chapter.

Chapter 5

A MODERN DILEMMA

Women's Rights

Generally speaking, women have been treated unfairly throughout history. Many of their sacrifices and labors have been unnoticed, forgotten, or never recorded—not only anciently, but also in our own dispensation. So it is no wonder that most of them feel inferior to men and feel they are not entitled to hold the Priesthood. In her Sunstone Symposium paper, Andrea Moore Emmett wrote:

> Yes, Mormon women know of those nameless pioneer women who broke their china into pieces for the Nauvoo Temple, bore and buried babies on the plains, and sacrificed their hearts to become plural wives. Mormon women know something of Emma and Lucy Mack Smith. But that's where it ends.
>
> Where are all those elusive faces and names of sisters and the individual, intimate stories of the lives they lived? They can be found in unreachable archives and the special collections at the B.Y.U. Library covered with the dust of unuse. The names and faces of women whose real life experiences parallel those of the men. Men whose bigger-than-life stories are told and retold as role models churchwide to our daughters as well as our sons. ("Subordination of Women Within the Latter-day Saint Church," Emmett, 1990 Sunstone Symposium paper, p. 2)

Many LDS women of today feel that they have become the victims of such sexual inequality and that they have lost their claim to Priesthood privileges and to many of their other deserved rights. Margaret Toscano holds the liberal opinion that Joseph Smith tried to rectify the situation and actually intended to give women the Priesthood:

> *Joseph Smith's great declaration of power and blessing to women and his attempt to extend the priesthood to them has been negated by a more recent, conservative reaction that has closed the doors of priesthood to women, leaving the rank and file members of the church to believe, generally, that priesthood is something that God does not want women to have. A majority of LDS women accept this tradition as doctrine. Any woman who stands forth to remind us of the true situation or to assert a desire for priesthood is likely to be stigmatized as unfaithful and power-hungry. ("Women in the Priesthood Hierarchy", Toscano, paper at First Mormon Women's Forum, p. 15)*

Nevertheless, a fairly universal disregard for women's rights and privileges has been going on throughout the pages of history; but because of women's efforts, their recognition has been improving. For example, in 1920 women won the right to vote with the passage of the 19th Amendment to the Constitution. The women's suffrage movement had labored for 72 years to obtain it, and now women were accepted as more a part of the male system in their social, political and religious activities. It was meant to help bring equality and unity to the male/female relationship. However, it may have produced more problems than it solved.

We have been taught the competitive system in our politics, business, religion and social activities until it has become a detriment instead of a benefit. Marriages have become so competitive that many of them conclude in divorce.

Our society has clamored for women's independence and equality so vehemently that it is producing more and more single people rather than encouraging compatible marriages. The feminist movements have demanded an "equality" that is leading women toward **freedom from** men, rather than **companions** to them.

Women's rights were slow getting out of the starting gate, even in Mormondom. With all the light and knowledge of the restoration, because of past traditions, women had difficulty in gaining the proper respect and rights they deserved; but when the Prophet Joseph Smith established the Women's Relief Society, an important break-through took place. Gradually the women were accepted into other organizations and even on the staff of Church publications, such as the **Young Women Journal,** the **Woman's Exponent,** and the **Relief Society Magazine.** Their pleas for recognition and rights were more often noticed and acted upon.

The "Woman Question" is the question of both man and woman; and "woman's rights" should as deeply interest men as women. Woman is the mother of the world, and her interests can no more be separated from those of man, than could the world exist with only one sex. It is to be hoped that this fact will have full weight in the future agitation of the "Woman Question." **(Woman's Exponent,** *Vol. 2, No. 1, June 1873, editorial)*

All honor and reverence to good men, but they and their attentions are not the only source of happiness on the earth, and need not fill up every thought of woman. And when men see that women can exist without them being constantly at hand, that they can learn to be self-reliant or depend upon each other for more or less happiness, it will perhaps take a little of the conceit out of some of them. ("Why, Ah, Why?" **Woman's Exponent,** *Sept. 30, 1874)*

Six weeks after the printing of the above article, the **Exponent** continued with the subject, commenting on the women's place both in the home and the workplace. It argued:

> It has been the popular cry that no woman could be a good, true, loving wife, and at the same time successfully follow any profession. If so, neither can a man do justice to any professional calling and prove a kind, affectionate, and loving husband. ("Heart vs. Head", **Women's Exponent**, Nov. 15, 1874, p. 92)

Brigham Young's opinion of women's rights seemed to get more liberal as time went on during his administration. In 1865 he stated:

> I am addressing myself to the ladies of the Kingdom of God, to those who know how to keep their houses, furniture and beds pure and clean, who can cook food for their husbands and children in a way that it will be clean, tasteful and wholesome. The woman that can do this I call a lady. In this view I differ from the world generally; for the lady of the world is not supposed to know anything about what is going on in the kitchen; her highest ambition is to be sure and be in the fashion, at no matter what cost to her husband or father; she considers that she may as well be out of the world as out of the fashion. (JD 11:138)

But in 1869, Brigham Young was encouraging women to develop their talents outside the home:

> As I have often told my sisters in the Female Relief Societies, we have sisters here who, if they had the privilege of studying, would make just as good mathematicians or accountants as any man; and we think they ought to have the privilege to study these branches of knowledge that they may develop the powers with which they are endowed. We believe that women are useful, not only to sweep houses, wash

dishes, make beds, and raise babies, but that they should stand behind the counter, study law or physics, or become good bookkeepers and be able to do the business in any counting house, and all this to enlarge their sphere of usefulness for the benefit of society at large. In following these things they but answer the design of their creation. (JD 13:61)

Thus, the status of Mormon women improved during Brigham Young's administration:

*His reorganization of the Relief Society launched women into an era of public activity that involved them in business and gave them new economic status in a community that was itself concerned with economic identity. Within MormonismÕs social order where women had previously held no offices, they gained position and visibility as leaders in organizations for women and children. **Though women were clearly not admitted to the priesthood, they began to share some of its influence over women** through disbursement of funds and counsel at general, stake, and ward levels. ("Woman's Place in Brigham Young's World," Jill Mulvay Derr, BYU Studies 18:3, Spring 1978, p. 394)*

The push for emergence of women into the workplace continued until its eventual realization, but then expanding areas of womenÕs liberation were desired— even requiring the changing of historical precedent and avowed orthodoxy.

But good things are often carried too far, as in the case of Sonja Johnson, whose activities attracted local and national media attention with her efforts to promote the Equal Rights Amendment. She encouraged "civil disobedience" and raised the pro-Equal Amendment flag above Temple Square along with her demonstrations. She labeled the LDS Church as the "arch-enemy of equal rights". Sonja explained the whole situation in her book **From Housewife to Heretic**.

Even though she was president of the "Mormons for ERA," she had been excommunicated from the Mormon Church. Sonja proposed "to give women the priesthood—and it will be the end of the church's patriarchy and the beginning of a new era." (**S.L. Tribune**, Mar. 19, 1982) She was also reported as saying:

> I just wish Mormon women would take advantage of their situation. They don't realize where they are, but they have the upper hand. They could push things a long way—if they would. * * *
>
> They've got the whip hand right now because church leaders are so afraid of what women might do. (**Ibid**.)

From her, many others took up the banner for women's rights, i.e., Carol Lynn Pearson:

> I want our children to know of the great lack of esteem for woman in the centuries after Christ, when Saint Clement said, "Every woman should be overwhelmed with shame at the very thought that she is a woman." To know that Saint Augustine denied women had souls and that this issue was debated at church councils. That Martin Luther said, "Woman, though a stupid vessel, is essential. But man must always hold power over her, for he is higher and better than she." I want them to be sad and angry for Saint Teresa of Avila who said, "The very thought that I am a woman is enough to make my wings droop."
>
> Our children need to know that 85 percent of those executed for witchcraft—hundreds of thousands, perhaps millions—were women whose sins were a show of rebellion or an evidence of spiritual power, seen as a threat to the male-dominated church and society. They should know that an ancient Moslem mosque still bears the inscription, "women and dogs and other impure animals are not permitted to enter." That in Morocco for centuries the custom was that the man rode the donkey and the woman walked six feet

behind—until WWII left many dangerous unexploded mines in the ground, after which the woman walked six feet in front of the donkey. That Chinese girl babies' feet were bound to keep them close to home and under complete male domination. That the phrase "rule of thumb" comes from old English law that dictates that a husband cannot beat his wife with a rod larger than his thumb. Our children need to know this sad history. And they need to know about brave women and men who struggled to change it. ("Healing the Motherless House," **Pearson, as quoted in** *Women and the Priesthood, Turner, pp. 237-38)*

Vella Neil Adams stated:

When Mormon women recognize that they are being defined by narrow, constrictive church images, some seek non-church avenues for identification and support. Some remain on church records but reduce their commitment and participation. Others feel damaged and suffer poor self-esteem or depression. ("Empowerment and Mormon Women's Publications", *Adams, Women and Authority, p. 64)*

Betina Lindsey explained:

Today, historical development has for the first time created the necessary conditions by which large groups of women, eventually all women, can emancipate themselves from subordination. This transforming of women's consciousness about ourselves and our thoughts is a precondition for change for all of society. Women can no longer wait for permission; they now must link hands and unitedly step forward of their own accord to rebalance the world and hail forth Zion. * * *

We are here to symbolically unlock the third millennia AD to the daughters of Eve. ("Eve 2000", *Lindsey, paper delivered at Mormon Women's Forum reception at the Lion House, May 16, 1989, pp. 2, 6)*

Generally speaking, the women of Utah have taken the greatest strides in defending their rights and freedoms. They have also shown their success in the work place. It is reported that they have made the greatest jump in the workplace because "more than 60% of the women in Utah work, more than in any other state. . . ." (**S.L. Tribune**, Mar. 11, 1990)

*Then what conclusion shall we arrive at? Why, consequently that the condition of woman today is much better in every respect than in the days of our grandmothers, and that the women of the future, will, judging from the outlook of the present, far surpass us who are now upon the stage of action. Woman is learning to think, act and reason for herself, not to hang her conscience on another, or pin her faith to the sleeve of anyone. Young girls are beginning to comprehend that employment, suited to the capacity of woman by which she may earn an independent living, is much more womanly than depending upon some male relative for maintenance and support. Besides many women are suddenly left helpless and alone, by the death of husband or father, and how desolate under such circumstances will she be who has never been taught self-dependence. This is one of the lessons thoughtful women are learning today, and it will be a legacy better than wealth, for it will not take wings and fly away. (**Contributor** 2:183)*

It would be well for more men to realize and appreciate the support and blessing of a good woman:

Strong-minded women are the very ones who will make the best aids and helpmeets for their husbands, competent to assist, advise and sympathize; and if men would interest themselves in helping to develop women's higher powers, instead of placing almost insurmountable barriers to hinder their progress, they would find it much to their own advantage; and women who are the most highly cultivated morally, mentally and religiously are the very ones to do honor and reverence to good men, who possess the noblest attributes and are the nearest akin to God and divinity. (Contributor 11:198)

The unfair and unequal treatment of women continues to diminish, and the "fairer sex" is coming more to the forefront. In the professional arena many women are proving themselves as capable and as aggressive as their male counterparts. Their achievements and successes clearly speak for themselves. For those women who want to expand their talents and abilities outside the home, there are increasing opportunities for them to do so.

However, with all these expanding rights and benefits for women, there are certain limits:

*And again, verily I say unto you, that the Son of Man cometh **not in the form of a woman**, . . . Wherefore, be not deceived. (D & C 49:22-23)*

As we look back, and then ahead, we ask, "How much good has come from all these efforts for "women's rights"? Awareness of the problem is fine, but often more problems and troubles result in trying to solve the problem. Sheila Graham commented on this:

For several decades women have been told if they want to get ahead in the business world, they must suppress their feminine traits and behave like men.

Women are different from men. Not better, not worse, different. Women look different, react differently, think differently—and that's all right. Feminine traits aren't inferior to masculine ones. They're complementary.

*Now, women have rights and choices. Women, how are you doing? Are you making the same mistakes so many men have made for thousands of years? ("What's Wrong with Women?", Graham, **Plain Truth**, pp. 12-13)*

Chapter 6

OUR MOTHER IN HEAVEN

Goddess Worship

As demands for women's rights have escalated, some women have begun to give too much respect, honor and even worship to others of their own sex. A new stage has been set for the worship of our Mother in Heaven because Father in Heaven is a man. Consider the following expressions of a few of today's women in this regard:

> *Jesus taught that doing the will of God is more important than formal worship. . . . If we want to worship the Mother, we must do the work of the Mother, and if we do the work of the Mother, we worship her. Her work is the same as his work. They are one God. . . . (Janice Allred, "Toward a Mormon Theology of God the Mother," quoted in Women and Authority, p. 275)*

> *If "like-begets-like", then we, as women, shall certainly never become like God the Father. To whom do we turn for our perfected identity? * * * I can't help but feel cheated about my lack of knowledge of "Her.: I wonder why she isn't allowed to speak, to guide and direct and console her daughters. (Karen Sorensen Smith, "Truth Is Reason, Truth Eternal", Dialogue IX:4, Winter 1974, p. 5)*

> *At our ward conference, our stake president said that in our stake there was a problem with praying*

*to the Mother in Heaven. He explained that there should be one authority or head of the church, one head of the stake, one head of the ward, one head of the family: in effect, if children don't know who's in charge, they get confused; having a female at the father's side creates confusion. He said that believing in the Mother or including Her in our prayers was of Satan. (Mary Olivia Stanton as quoted in "Emerging Discourse on the Divine Feminine," **Women and Authority**, pp. 259-60)*

*In and out of Mormonism, men have identified with the gender of God the Father. In Mormonism there is a literal identification between their bodies and the body of God. And now women have begun to identify with God the Mother. It is an empowering experience to see your body in the body of God. . . . Some of us pray to a mother god because we believe she is talking to us. (Lynne Kanavel Whitesides, "Finding Our Bodies, Hearts, Voices. . ." U of U, May 1992, quoted in **Women and Authority**, p. 261)*

Mr. Tom Snyder joined the mother-worship program by delivering a written prayer for the Salt Lake City Council. He wanted to drop all prayer from any government meeting as a means of separation of church and state. He delivered a draft of his prayer to the City Council which is as follows:

Our Mother in heaven. . . We fervently ask that you guide the leaders of Salt Lake City . . . and Utah, so that they may see the wisdom of separating church and state and so that they will never again perform demeaning religious ceremonies as part of official government functions, . . .

*We pray that you prevent self-righteous politicians from misusing the name of God in conducting government meetings; and, that you lead them away from the hypocritical and blasphemous deception of the public. (**S.L. Tribune**, Jan. 19, 1994)*

On September 7, 1991, the Salt Lake Chapter of Mormon Women's Forum held a meeting on "How Should We Worship God the Mother." It began by a reading of excerpts from Pres. Gordon B. Hinckley's address given in April 1991 to the regional representatives seminar. He was instructing the Elders not to allow the Saints to pray to a mother in heaven. The four panelists on this occasion presented differing opinions, with Rodney Turner quoted as saying—

> . . . that although the meeting's title presupposed that worshipping Mother is appropriate, there is no justification in the gospel setting for it. * * * He said Mother worship has its roots in pagan sex and fertility rites and ritual prostitution. He said Moses spoke against it and that it reappeared in Catholic worship of Mary. If praying to Mother is so important, why wasn't it revealed in the Restoration?", he asked.
>
> Turner said that to continue to pray to Mother after the prophet and the first Presidency have said not to, is to "rationalize yourself to apostasy." You can't get ahead of the prophet. . . . "Satan will carefully lead you to hell, singing praises to our Mother in Heaven." (**Sunstone**, Oct. 1991, p. 60)

At an earlier symposium, a similar condemnation had been vocalized—

> A cover-up was exposed at BYU's J. Reuben Clark Law School recently. Several speakers at the 32nd Annual Symposium on the Archaeology of the Scriptures . . . pointed accusing fingers back through time. They held two groups of people responsible for "covering up" valuable information about ancient Hebrew goddess worship. . . . Dr. Raphael Patai, renowned Hebraist and anthropologist, said "**Goddesses** were worshipped most of the time by most Jewish people, even in the temple . . . but the Bible writers . . . only refer to it as **idolatry and condemn it as utter abomination.**" (**Church News**, Oct. 30, 1983, p. 7)

We are witnesses of further appeals made by both men and women who are asking for a "new consciousness," a "mass awareness of the new truths" that "herald the need for change" because they [women] can give a better "example and leadership" through their "sensitivities." (J. E. Chapman's paper, "Dissent in the Church," n.d., p. 15)

Apparently some of the Jews fell into the worship of a mother in heaven:

> *Christ kept his first estate; Lucifer lost his by offering to save men in their sins on the honor of a God, or on his father's honor. . . . Christ hated sin and loved righteousness; therefore, he was anointed with holy oil in heaven, and crowned in the midst of virtue, and smiled upon a Son that kept the faith as the heir of all things! In fact, the Jews thought so much of this coronation among gods and goddesses, Kings and Queens of heaven, that they broke over all restraints and actually began to worship the "Queen of Heaven," according to Jeremiah. (W. W. Phelps, T & S, 5:758)*

The Jews told Jeremiah that they would continue to—

> *. . . burn incense unto the queen of heaven [because when they did it] then we had plenty of victuals, and were well, and saw no evil. But since we left off to burn incense to the queen of heaven, and to pour out drink offerings unto her, we have wanted all things and have been consumed by the sword and by the famine." (Jer. 44:17-18)*

It sounds like a good argument in favor of worshipping the "Queen of Heaven"; however, Jeremiah didn't buy it. He warned them that because they did vow to the queen of heaven and make offerings to her (among other things), the Lord had said, "Behold, I will watch over them for evil, and not for good; and all the men of Judah that are in the land of Egypt shall be consumed by the sword and by famine until there be an end of them." (**Ibid.**, v. 27)

The Jews were not the only ones involved in the worship of a mother in heaven. It was soon taken up by Catholics. It was not a part of the worship in the New Testament, but it soon followed. The historian John W. Draper wrote:

> *Nestor was deeply imbued with the doctrines of Aristotle, and attempted to coordinate them with what he considered the orthodox Christian tenets. Between him and Cyril, the Bishop or Patriarch of Alexandria, a quarrel accordingly arose. Cyril represented the paganizing, Nestor the philosophizing party of the Church. This was the Cyril who had murdered Hypatia. Cyril determined that the worship of the Virgin as the Mother of God should be recognized, Nestor was determined that it should not. In a sermon delivered in the metropolitan church at Constantinople, he vindicated the attributes of the Eternal, the Almighty God. "And can this God have a mother?" he exclaimed. In other sermons and writings, he set forth with more precision his ideas that the Virgin should be considered not as the Mother of God, but as the mother of the human portion of Christ, that portion being as essentially distinct from the divine as is a temple from its contained deity.*
>
> *Initiated by the monks of Alexandria, the monks of Constantinople took up arms in behalf of "the Mother of God." The quarrel rose to such a pitch that the emperor was constrained to summon a council to meet at Ephesus.* (**Conflict between Religion and Science**, *p. 71*)

Out of these conflicts and suppositions came the doctrine of Mariology and Mariolatry. This was a form of feminine worship that seemingly arose from the ashes of the apostate Egyptians in their worship of Isis, a deity that eventually was relegated into the realm of deities among the spiritually ignorant Romans and Greeks.

There was also the worship of Ceres, another matriarch, who came into being along with other ancient mothers of the gods:

> *The entire silence of history respecting the worship of the Virgin down to the end of the fourth century, proves clearly that it was foreign to the original spirit of Christianity, and belongs among the many innovations of the post-Nicene age.*
>
> ***In the beginning of the fifth century,*** *however, the worship of saints appeared in full bloom, and then* ***Mary, by reason of her singular relation to the Lord, was soon placed at the head. . . . (History of the Christian Church,*** *Schaff, 3:422-23)*

Another part of this worship of Mary over Christ was the introduction of the Candlemass which was a festival introduced by Pope Gelasius in 494. With lighted candles there was a procession of marching and singing as they walked out of the church and through the city as a ceremonial purification of the Virgin Mary forty days after the birth of Jesus. This came on the 2nd of February and was also a part of the memorial to Jesus who was presented at the temple where he met Simeon and Anna.

After 650 A.D. a ceremony was initiated called the Nativity of Mary. After the 9th century another festival was started called the Presentation of Mary. At the time of Origin (4th century) some believed and taught that Mary had suffered martyrdom, which further catapulted her veneration. (See Luke 2:34-35.)

From the 13th century—

> . . . *the* ***Ave Maria*** *stands in the Roman church upon a level with the Lord's Prayer and the Apostles' Creed, and with them forms the basis of the rosary. (**History of the Christian Church** Schaff, 3:425)*

And the 19th century—

> . . . *the festival of the Immaculate Conception, which arose with the doctrine of the sinless conception of Mary, and is interwoven with the history of that dogma down to its official and final promulgation by Pope Pius IX in 1854. (**Ibid.**, 3:428)*

The Catholic Church displays more statues and paintings of the Madonna than of Christ; and the prayers of intercession are directed more to the Mother than to the Son or Father. It marks a cardinal difference between the Catholic and Protestant world, and is also another instance of pushing a mortal person between man and God.

Along this line, there is an interesting account of the Catholic Church even having a woman pope for over two years:

> *And again, admitting that the Priesthood remained intact till the time of Pope Joan, the chain certainly must have been broken then; for it is known that she obtained the stool under the disguise of a man, and the trick was not discovered till an illegitimate young Pope was born, the result of a criminal intercourse with a domestic. Pope Joan, or Pope John VIII, as she styled herself, died on giving birth to this child, having held the popedom two years, one month and two days. Now, it is not supposable that she held a Priesthood, for we have no account in Holy Writ that God ever intended that a woman should be the head of the Church. ("The Priesthood—Where Is It, or Who Has It?", Elder William W. Riter,* **Mill. Star***, 27:818, Dec. 1865)*

The scriptures speak of her as "the mother of the Lord" but that has now become "the mother of God". Her true place in scripture is modestly in the background, and events surrounding her birth and death are unknown. After the fourth century it was taught that she was a married virgin, a wife never touched by her husband and dedicated to a perpetual purity and virginity. The doctrine of the Immaculate Conception of Mary was for the first time announced in 1140 A.D. at Lyons, but became an issue between the Franciscans and the Dominicans until established by a Papal decree in 1854.

The historian Phillip Schaff described some of the historical background:

> *From this Mariology follows Mariolatry. If Mary is, in the strict sense of the word, the mother of God, it seems to follow as a logical consequence, that she herself is divine, and therefore an object of divine worship.* * * *

> *The first instance of the formal invocation of Mary occurs in the prayers of Ephraim Syrus (379 AD), addressed to Mary and the saints, and attributed by the tradition of the Syrian church. . . .*

> *The first more certain example appears in Gregory Nazianzen (389 AD), who, in his eulogy on Cyprian, relates of Justina that she besought the virgin Mary to protect her threatened virginity. . . . (Ibid., 3:422)*

In His day, Jesus continually opposed and warned against the "traditions" of His society. This warning should be heeded today as well, for such traditions can be very devastating to a religion. They are often merged with the central themes of local religions, almost without the people knowing what has happened.

Eugene England painted a clear picture of these dangerous influences and how they can work even in the Mormon Church:

> *[Certain beliefs] are imported from the prevailing culture. Then what seem like supportive ideas from*

> *Mormon doctrine or practices of the Church are combined with the cultural beliefs and the combination given authoritative support by statements of some Church leaders or religion teachers. These statements are usually tentative or merely personal at first, but as they are repeated they become more dogmatic and semi-official until they become independent of the persons who first tentatively expressed them and are accepted as official doctrine by many or even most of the Church—though they are not accepted by all Church leaders and may, in fact, be directly repudiated by at least some. ("Are All Alike Unto God?", **Sunstone**, April 1990, p. 24)*

The worship of our Mother in Heaven is only one of many doctrinal issues that individual members have tried to introduce into the Church. Others have come through social or political influences. As pressure mounts over an issue from outside and/or inside the Church, it frequently has been accepted as authoritative and official—even as the will of the Lord.

At a recent conference for women in Minnesota, for which several churches contributed hundreds of thousands of dollars, the following April 1994 news item was released, mentioning their worship of a female goddess:

> *The Church of England's ordination of 32 priestesses last month may have grabbed the headlines—and ended all hope of bridging the centuries-old rift between Canterbury and Rome—but American seismographs were picking up a different rumble.*
>
> *"The fallout from last fall's `Re-Imagining' event,"* reports this month's **Christianity Today**, *"has continued to escalate as more people have discovered the depth of its unorthodox feminist worship and teaching."*
>
> *Participants in the conference, held last November in Minneapolis, were told to seek inspiration from*

pantheistic religions and the gnostic gospels, and prayers were offered to Sophia, a wisdom goddess that some apostates associate with the Creation.

"Our maker, Sophia, we are women in your image," feminist leaders chanted. "With our warm body fluids we remind the world of its pleasures and sensations."

"I don't think we need folks hanging on crosses and blood dripping and weird stuff," said feminist theologian Delores Williams.

The event was funded by, among others, the Presbyterian Church USA, Church Women United, the United Methodist Church, the Evangelical Lutheran Church of America and the American Baptist Church. Not all members of these bodies, it is said, are pleased. (**Arizona Republic**, *by William Cheshire, April 12, 1994)*

What a strange historical review! As apostasy rears its ugly head, the false doctrines of the past come with it. The Mormon Church, unfortunately, is not exempt from such temptations and influences.

The King and Queen of Heaven

From ancient history to the present time, there is a continuous record of the most exalted station of women. Among men and among Gods, she holds a rightful place and an equal position, even to holding and sharing the blessings and rights of the Holy Priesthood—but she is not to be worshipped.

The greatest revelations and manifestations assuring us of a mother in heaven were revealed in this last dispensation; however, none of these instructed us to pray to her or to worship her, as Orson Pratt clearly explained:

But if we have a heavenly Mother as well as a heavenly Father, is it not right that we should worship the

*Mother of our spirits as well as the Father? No; for the Father of our spirits is at the head of His household, and His wives and children are required to yield the most perfect obedience to their great Head. **It is lawful for the children to worship the King of Heaven,** but not the "Queen of Heaven." The children of Israel were severely reproved for making offerings to the "Queen of Heaven." Although she is highly exalted and honored as the beloved bride of the great King, yet the children, so far as we are informed, **have never been commanded to pray to her or worship her.** Jesus prayed to His Father, and taught His disciples to do likewise; but we are nowhere taught that Jesus prayed to His heavenly Mother: neither did he pray to the Holy Ghost as his Father. (**The Seer**, p. 159)*

The Lord's Prayer was given us as an example of how to pray:

After this manner therefore pray ye: Our Father which art in heaven, Hallowed be thy name. Thy kingdom come, Thy will be done in earth, as it is in heaven. (Matt. 6:9-10)

This prayer clearly directs us to pray to one person, "Our Father," and ask for **His** [masculine, singular] will to be done.

Another excellent example showing to whom we should direct our prayers, comes from the popular poem/hymn, "Invocation," wherein Eliza R. Snow addresses her Father in Heaven:

*Oh my Father, thou that dwellest
In the high and glorious place,
When shall I regain thy presence,
And again behold thy face?*
(LDS Hymns, p. 139)

Once again, our Heavenly Father is the only one being addressed, and certainly Eliza learned about the Godhead and how to pray from her husband, Joseph Smith. In the third stanza of this hymn, she acknowledges the existence of a mother in heaven, but yet she is not praying to her.

Though we have not been directed to pray to our Mother in heaven, she probably has much more to do with us and our salvation than we perceive. More and more is being revealed or discovered to support that ideal. From an early Christian writing found recently called "The Pearl," several quotations give us further light on this interesting subject. Dr. Hugh Nibley relates the following comforting passage from that "Pearl":

> *The Christian comes to earth from his heavenly home, leaving his royal parents behind, for a period of testing upon the earth. Then having overcome the dragon, he returns to the heavenly place, where he is given a rousing welcome. The first person to greet him on his return is his **heavenly mother**, who was the last one to embrace him as he left to go down to earth. (**Old Testament and Related Studies**, Nibley, p. 90)*

Not only is Eve the mother of our mortal bodies, but also of our spiritual bodies, as explained by Brigham Young:

> *And **Eve, our common mother, who is the mother of all living, bore these spirits in the Celestial world**, and then this earth was organized by Elohim, Jehovah, and Michael, who is Adam, our common Father.*
>
> *Adam and Eve had the privilege to continue the work of progression, consequently came to this earth and commenced the great work of forming tabernacles for those spirits to dwell in. (Brigham Young, **L. John Nuttall Journal**, 1:19)*

Certainly our Mother Eve is very concerned about the comings and goings of her spirit children on this mortal earth, as this is an important part of her stewardship. Recently a midwife in Central Utah had a spiritual experience during a rather difficult homebirth. During a brief moment of serious concern for the safe arrival of the baby and wanting special guidance, she silently asked Mother Eve, "Please let your mind be my mind, and your hands my hands." She immediately knew what she needed to do, and her hands felt as if they were being guided by greater hands than her own. How could there be anything improper in such a sincere petition!

With all the due respect that we should have for our Mother in heaven, there is still a definite order and pattern regarding the roles of men and women in this world, and so it is in the eternal world.

In summary, then—

1.   The scriptures inform us that Eve was taken from man—a part of him. Though a figurative description, it still denotes the pattern for male/female relationship and status that exists on this world as well as the worlds to come.

2.   Jesus gave us the example and said to pray to our Father in heaven. If   it was correct to pray to our Heavenly Mother, He would have said so.

3.   Praying to a Mother in heaven was never part of the teachings or examples of any ancient or latter-day prophets.

4.   Praying to a Mother in heaven or a female goddess originated as a pagan rite and was never a part of worship in Israel.

According to scripture and revelation, sufficient respect, reverence and devotion can be offered to our Heavenly Mother without praying to her.

Chapter 7

CHURCH OFFICES

Appendages to the Priesthood

According to the Doctrine and Covenants, church offices are appendages to "the Holy Priesthood, after the Order of the Son of God"—or Melchizedek Priesthood:

> *There are, in the church, two priesthoods, namely, the Melchizedek and Aaronic, including the Levitical Priesthood. Why the first is called the Melchizedek Priesthood is because Melchizedek was such a great high priest. Before his day it was called the Holy Priesthood, after the Order of the Son of God. But out of respect or reverence to the name of the Supreme Being, to avoid the too frequent repetition of his name, they, the church, in ancient days, called that priesthood after Melchizedek, or the Melchizedek Priesthood. **All other authorities or offices in the church are appendages to this priesthood**. (D & C 107:1-5)*

However, Section 84 does clarify that certain offices are **necessary** appendages to the Priesthood:

> *And again, the offices of elder and bishop are **necessary** appendages belonging unto the high priesthood. And again, the offices of teacher and deacon are **necessary** appendages belonging to the lesser priesthood, which priesthood was confirmed upon Aaron and his sons. (D & C 84:29-30)*

It is through this Priesthood authority that the LDS Church and all offices in it were established—signifying that the Priesthood is greater than the Church or any of its offices, or, in other words, the creator is greater than its creation.

Who has held these Priesthood offices?

*From the time the priesthood was restored to Joseph Smith its **offices** were available only to males. Like their Puritan counterparts two centuries earlier, Mormon women found themselves at the bottom of a hierarchically ordered system. The Mormon order extended from the First Presidency, with the responsibility of governing the entire Church, through stake presidents and bishops with governmental responsibility for specific geographic regions, to the individual father whose priesthood responsibility was righteous government of his family. Women assumed the responsibility for governing children and for heading households in the absence of their husbands, a frequent occurrence in Mormon society. This divinely designated order did not necessarily imply that females were intellectually or spiritually inferior to males. Brigham Young himself acknowledged "that many women are smarter than their husbands" (JD 9:39), though it was "not the privilege of a woman to dictate the husband." (JD 17:159) ("Woman's Place in Brigham Young's World," Jill Mulvay Derr, **BYU Studies** 18:3, Spring 1978, pp. 380-81)*

Neither did Linda Newell find references to women holding these offices.

I have not found recorded cases where women themselves have claimed ordination to priesthood office. There are, however, accounts of women being "ordained" to specific callings and of women who exercised powers and spiritual gifts now assigned only to men who hold the priesthood. These practices and their endorsement by such church leaders as Joseph Smith,

Brigham Young, John Taylor, Heber J. Grant, and oth-
ers, have left the unanswered question of what authori-
ty women are intended to hold. ("The Historical
Relationship of Mormon Women and Priesthood,"
*Newell, **Women and Authority**, Hanks, pp. 23-24)*

The Lord does not usually give dictatorial mandates to
the LDS Church (as He does with the Priesthood) without the voice and vote of the members. They have the
option as to whether or not to sustain Church officers
and leaders, doctrines and programs. They have the
right to vote in or sustain any color, sex or nationality as
part of their membership and officers. Unfortunately,
however, today a negative vote may mean the sacrifice of
one's temple recommend or Church membership. In fact,
at the October 1994 solemn assembly session of General
Conference, President Gordon B. Hinckley instructed
stake presidencies to report any negative votes directly to
the First Presidency—which would probably result in
some type of disciplinary action for the involved mem-
ber(s).

Joseph Fielding Smith once said, "The Church of
Jesus Christ of Latter-day Saints is the most democratic institution in the world." (**Imp. Era** 21:100) The First
Presidency even reiterated this in the 1970-71 course of
study for the Melchizedek Priesthood quorums. (p. 103)
However, this is a debatable statement, since most deci-
sions are made by Church leaders without any vote from
its members.

For example, one particular program change occurred
in 1902 when Church leaders, without calling for a vote
from the membership, decided to send 27 lady missionaries out in the field, two by two, just as the Elders were
going. (See **Messages of the First Presidency** 3:50.) No
administrations, ordinations or baptisms were to be performed by them, but they held the office or calling of a fulltime
missionary. These callings have gradually increased up to the
present time with an average of about 20% of LDS Church

missionaries being women. At times the percentage would go as high as 40%. (See "A History of Female Missionary Activity, 1830-1898," by Calvin Kunz, BYU thesis)

Occasionally, when a vote has been called, dissenting votes against a prospective office holder have had an influence on the final outcome. Thus, the Church may be considered as somewhat democratic.

The Priesthood, on the other hand, does not derive its power or validity from the vote of Church members. Its principles and laws come from God and are eternal, and if individuals vote against them, they are condemning themselves not the Priesthood. Nevertheless, God and Christ do not impose tyranny on any of their subjects.

In the early years of the Church it was repeatedly taught that endowed and married women held the Priesthood in **connection with their husbands** and had the same rights, blessings, powers and privileges; but gradually the expression of that point of view was discouraged and suppressed. In recent years, however, that teaching has been rediscovered, and many women are clamoring for those rights again. The problem is understanding the correct nature and exercise of this Priesthood. Some women want it conferred on them with the subsequent ordination to a Priesthood office in the Church. Even some men have supported this position, such as James Chapman who wrote:

> *Mormon males are taught from infancy that the priesthood will be given to them by a just, kind and loving father in heaven as one of the most desirable and useful gifts they could ever possess in this life and throughout eternity. Females are taught that God wasn't referring to them, that He has made them unacceptable (as human beings) to hold priesthood office.* * * *

What effect does it have on a woman's image of herself when she is instructed that no matter what she does she cannot gain equal status with men in the eyes of God? What is her reaction to this message? Will it inspire her to do good, to love God, to be at peace with herself and others? And what of the men throughout her lifetime who convey this message to her? Will they be filled with love, humility and compassion? Will a deep sense of human equality and empathy guide their involvement with women?

*What does it do to a woman, a young girl, to hear over and over again in so many ways, and at all times, that because she is female, she has been denied by God and made unqualified to hold priesthood as men can? What does it do to a woman's sense of her own worth to know that in the most important realm of her life she is not valued as men are valued, and will never have the same chances and opportunities as they will have? (**S.L. Tribune**, Sept. 2, 1990)*

Mr. Chapman concedes that his frustration would be lessened by giving women the same offices in the Church that male members are entitled to. He concluded:

Optimistically, however, a new and promising perspective is beginning to surface. A growing number of Latter-day Saints now feel that lack of priesthood office should in no way preclude female participation in all governing units of the modern church.

*Talented and loving women will be as effective in Mormon bishoprics, stake presidencies, high councils and in the ranks of general authorities as males will be. (**Ibid**.)*

Other public voices have supported the same proposition, i.e. Edwin Firmage:

University of Utah law professor Edwin Firmage says there is no doctrinal basis for the Mormon Church's restriction against women holding the church's priesthood or other authoritative offices.

"Within my own religious tradition, I long for that time when four black people, three of them women, will sit on the stand as general authorities at general conference," said Mr. Firmage, referring to offices in the LDS Church that currently only men may hold.

"No reason exists in Mormon doctrine, I believe, to prevent full priesthood participation by women with every office and calling in the church being open to them," he said at the annual Monsignor McDougall Lecture at the Cathedral of the Madeleine.

*"Imagine—four black (Mormon) general authorities, three of them female," he said. "This profound visual message of healing would transcend in immediate healing power every sermon ever given in our holy house, the Mormon Tabernacle." (**S.L. Tribune**, Mar. 9, 1989)*

With this approach, Mr. Firmage is taking an opposite view from prophets, patriarchs and apostles of the past 6,000 years. He concludes with his own view of how he is reconciled to God, which sounds more confusing than sensible:

*Reconciliation with God comes from introspection, understanding others, and correcting injustices. "Within my own soul I become male and female, Mormon and Catholic, Jew, Moslem and Hindu, Russian and American, black, brown and white," he said. (**Ibid.**)*

Paul likens the church to a human body, each person being a vital part of that church and all are necessary for it to function properly. Women are a part of that church body—perhaps the inner part that is not so visible, but their functions and contributions are just as necessary as any other part.

Paul says that the eye cannot say to the hand, "I have no need of thee," nor can any part say that it has no need of any of the other parts. (See I Cor. 12:14-23) It is also necessary to understand that one part cannot desire to be some other part.

The rib cannot say that she wants to be the arm, or the eye or the head. Whatever the calling that God gives us, we should be satisfied with it. Thus, a woman should graciously accept the fact that—

> Her "priesthood" callings are not elder, bishop, seventy or apostle—but wife, mother, teacher and comforter. These are at least as important and demanding as any of those exercised by men. (Rodney Turner, **Woman and the Priesthood**, p. 286)

Priesthood never has been just a badge, title, rank, position or office, but rather authority, leadership and rule, that when exercised righteously is a guide and influence in the family—showing the way back to Our Heavenly Father's presence.

Governing the Church

Churches may grow, prosper, and do great missionary service in the name of Christ, but they may or may not be governed by Priesthood. They can lose it more easily than they gained it.

When church leaders call people to hold offices in its organization, they may or may not be inspired to make those choices. Those calls to offices and missions usually come from the organization; the power and authority of Priesthood comes from God. Hence, there is usually an eventual separation between church and priesthood. Men are called to offices, but the gifts, powers, and revelations to magnify those callings come through the power of God. When the division between church offices and priesthood callings becomes too great, it becomes obvious—as Margaret Toscano stated:

> Some Mormon women want nothing to do with the hierarchal priesthood system that operates the modern

church. They see priesthood leadership as power-centered and corruptible. ("Put On Your Strength. . ." **Women and Authority**, *p. 418)*

Too often the Priesthood is used as a means for position, gain or authority over people instead of a power to purify and bring souls to God. It should not make dictators out of men, but rather make them more understanding and charitable. If Priesthood is used to gain power or authority over people, then its spirituality becomes dead, the gifts are lost, and the Priesthood departs. Nothing is left but the vanity and unrighteous dominion of man.

God has established that revelation should be directed to men for the governing of the Priesthood and its quorums in the Church. Joseph F. Smith called our attention to this:

*I want to tell you another thing: Our Heavenly Father has never yet to my knowledge revealed to this Church any great principle through a woman. Now, sisters, do not cast me off or deny the faith, because I tell you that God has never revealed any great and essential truth for the guidance of the Latter-day Saints through any woman. "Oh! but," says one, "What about Eliza Snow's beautiful hymn, `O My Father, Thou that dwellest,' etc.? Did not the Lord reveal through her that great and glorious principle that we have a mother as well as a father in heaven?" No. God revealed that principle to Joseph Smith; Joseph Smith revealed it to Eliza Snow Smith, his wife; and Eliza Snow was inspired, being a poet, to put it into verse. If we give anybody on earth credit for that, we give it to the Prophet Joseph Smith. But first of all we give it to God, who revealed it to His servant the Prophet. God reveals Himself and His truths through the channels of the Priesthood. (**Collected Discourses**, 4:229, Jan. 20, 1895)*

The **Times and Seasons** editor had previously noted this in 1840:

> *The piece further states that "a woman preacher appointed a meeting at New Salem, Ohio, and in the meeting read and repeated copious extracts from the* **Book of Mormon.***" Now it is a fact well known, that we have not had a female preacher in our connection, for we do not believe in a female priesthood. (***T & S***, 1:46)*

But this policy is definitely opposed by some women today, such as Andrea Emmett, who feels women should be entitled to hold Priesthood offices in the Church:

> *There are no female Apostles, female Seventies, female high councilors, priestesses, female bishops, stake, mission, quorum, or Sunday School presidents, etc. Directives from the Women's General Auxiliary leaders to the female membership are addressed "Dear Brethren" and signed by the First Presidency. Male leaders make all the policies and decisions on every level for all members, male and female. With their totally male perspective, they write, define, and expound on what it means to be, and how to be, a woman. ("Subordination of Women within the Latter-day Saint Church", p. 4, Emmett, Sunstone Symposium panel discussion, 1990)*

Let's see what the Prophet Joseph Smith had to say about this concept. When he learned about a church organization called the Irvingites, he said, "The Irvingites are a people that have counterfeited the truth, perhaps the nearest of any of our modern sectarians." (TPJS, p. 210) They had apostles, prophets, teachers, etc., and professed having some spiritual gifts. On one of Mr. Irving's journeys in Scotland, he met "some Misses Campbell" who had the gift of "utterances," and when they were introduced into Mr. Irving's church in London, they were termed "prophetesses of God". They organized the church and when they spoke, Mr. Irving and his ministers had to keep silent. The Prophet clearly explained the reasons why Mr. Irving's church was not of God:

> It may be asked, where is there anything in all this that is wrong?
> First. **The church was organized by women**, and God placed in the Church (first apostles, secondarily prophets,) and not first women; but Mr. Irving placed in his church first women (secondarily apostles,) and the church was founded and organized by them. **A woman has no right to found or organize a church—God never sent them to do it.**
> Second. **Those women would speak in the midst of a meeting, and rebuke Mr. Irving or any of the church**. Now the scripture positively says, "Thou shalt not rebuke an Elder, but entreat him as a father;" not only this, but they frequently accused the brethren, thus placing themselves in the seat of Satan, who is emphatically called "the accuser of the brethren." (TPJS, p. 212)

Joseph Smith also similarly criticized a church organized by Johanna Southcott, who claimed to be a prophetess. She wrote a book about her prophecies in 1804, and her church was still active at the time Joseph spoke of it.

> She [Johanna Southcott] was to bring forth, in a place appointed, a son, that was to be the Messiah, which thing has failed. Independent of this, however, **where do we read of a woman that was the founder of a church, in the word of God**? Paul told the women in his day, "To keep silence in the church, and that if they wished to know anything to ask their husbands at home;" he would not suffer a woman "to rule, or to usurp authority in the church;" but here we find a woman the founder of a church, the revelator and guide, the Alpha and Omega, contrary to all **acknowledged rule, principle, and order**. (TPJS, p. 209)

Apparently this same warning and caution should be taken regarding any woman starting churches, such as the famous Ann Lee of the Quakers, and more recently the pillar of the Seventh Day Adventists, Ellen G. White.

Brigham Young also cautioned:

> When the servants of God in any age have consented to follow a woman for a leader, either in a public or a family capacity, they have sunk beneath the standard their organization has fitted them for; when a people of God submit to that, **their Priesthood is taken from them,** and they become as any other people. (JD 9:308)

The holding of a particular office in the Church is not necessarily an indication of the possession of Priesthood. Offices merely signify appendages, callings, functions, missions or types of work; they do not reflect or measure the amount of Priesthood a person has. For instance, if a person receives the Melchizedek Priesthood, then any office in the Church or Priesthood will never give him any more Priesthood—it just provides him the opportunity or calling of using his Priesthood in whatever function that office requires.

Though very rare, a man holding the Priesthood may have no office in the Church at all, but no office does not necessarily mean he has no Priesthood. For example, when the Aaronic Priesthood was conferred upon Joseph Smith and Oliver Cowdery in May 1829, John the Baptist made no mention of ordaining them to any office within that Priesthood:

> Upon you my fellow servants, in the name of Messiah, I confer the Priesthood of Aaron, which holds the keys of the ministering of angels, and of the gospel of repentance, and of baptism by immersion for the

*remission of sins; and this shall never be taken again from the earth until the sons of Levi do offer again an offering unto the Lord in righteousness. (**P of GP**, Jos. Smith 2:69)*

It was not until after the Church was organized in April of 1830 that they held an **office** in the Priesthood or Church.

According to Michael Quinn, it is similarly possible for a woman to hold the Priesthood and yet not be ordained to any office in it:

Priesthood exists independently of church offices, but church offices are appendages which cannot exist without the priesthood. * * *

***A woman does not need an appendage to have priesthood**. According to Joseph Smith's teachings to the Relief Society and to the Anointed Quorum, a woman receives Melchizedek priesthood when she receives the endowment. The confusion of priesthood office with priesthood has characterized many contemporary discussions of women and priesthood.*

*However, just as counselors in the First Presidency were "ordained" by Joseph Smith, Emma Smith was "ordained to expound the Scriptures," (DHC 4:553) and "her counselors were ordained" to preside over the Nauvoo Relief Society. In the nineteenth century the word "ordain" was also used for appointing persons to proselyting missions and to heal. However, **I find no evidence that Mormon men ever ordained a woman to a specific priesthood office of the church**. ("Mormon Women Have Had the Priesthood Since 1843," Quinn, **Women and Authority**, p. 375)*

Quinn also said, "For LDS women, Melchizedek Priesthood does not come in stages of ordination, but in the temple endowment." (**Ibid**., p. 384) This will be discussed in the next chapter.

Chapter 8

THE TEMPLE ENDOWMENT

The Significance of the Endowment

Included as an introduction to this chapter is an excerpt from a sermon given by Brigham Young in the Salt Lake Tabernacle, April 6, 1853 (when the cornerstone for the S.L. Temple was laid), wherein he emphasized the importance of temples and the endowment:

Soon after [the restoration], the Church, through our beloved Prophet Joseph, was commanded to build a Temple to the Most High in Kirtland, Ohio, and this was the next House of the Lord we hear of on the earth, since the days of SolomonŌs Temple. Joseph not only received revelation and commandment to build a temple, but he received a pattern also, as did Moses for the Tabernacle and Solomon for his Temple; for without a pattern, he could not know what was wanting, having never seen one, and not having experienced its use.

Without revelation, Joseph could not know what was wanting, any more than any other man, and, without commandment, the Church were too few in numbers, too weak in faith, and too poor in purse, to attempt such a mighty enterprise. but by means of all these stimulants, a mere handful of men, living on air, and a little hominy and milk, and often salt or no salt when milk could not be had; the great Prophet Joseph, in the stone quarry, quarrying rock with his own hands; and the few men in the Church, following his example of obedience and diligence wherever most needed; with laborers on the walls, holding the sword in one hand to protect themselves from the mob, while they placed the stone and moved the trowel with the other, the Kirtland Temple, the second House of the Lord that we have any published record of on the earth, was so far completed as to be dedicated. And those first Elders who helped to build it, received a portion of their first endowments, or we might say more clearly, some of the first, or introductory, or initiatory ordinances preparatory to an endowment.

The preparatory ordinances there administered, though accompanied by the ministration of angels, and the presence of the Lord Jesus, were but a faint similitude of the ordinances of the House of the Lord in their fullness; yet many, through the instigation of the devil, thought they had received all, and knew as much as God; they have apostatized, and gone to hell. but be assured, brethren, there are but few, very few of the Elders of Israel, now on earth, who know the meaning of the word endowment. To know, they must experience; and to experience, a Temple must be built.

Let me give you the definition in brief. Your endowment is to receive all those ordinances in the House of the Lord, which are necessary for you, after you have departed this life, to enable you to walk back to the presence of the Father, passing the angels who stand as sentinels, being enabled to give them the key words, the signs and tokens, pertaining to the Holy Priesthood, and gain your eternal exaltation in spite of earth and hell.

Who has received and understands such an endowment in this assembly? You need not answer. Your voices would be few and far between, yet the keys to these endowments are among you, and thousands have received them, so that the devil, with all his aids, need not suppose he can again destroy the Holy Priesthood from the earth, by killing a few, for he cannot do it. God has set His hand, for the last time, to redeem His people, the honest in heart, and Lucifer cannot hinder Him.

Before these endowments could be given at Kirtland, the Saints had to flee before mobocracy. And, by toil and daily labor, they found places in Missouri, where they laid the cornerstones of Temples, in Zion and her stakes, and then had to retreat to Illinois, to save the lives of those who could get away alive from Missouri, where fell the Apostle David W. Patten, with many like associates, and where they were imprisoned in loathsome dungeons, and fed on human flesh, Joseph and Hyrum, and many others. But before this had transpired, the Temple at Kirtland had fallen into the hands of wicked men, and by them been polluted, like the Temple at Jerusalem, and consequently it was disowned by the Father and the Son. At Nauvoo, Joseph dedicated another Temple, the third on record. He knew what was wanting, for he had previously given most of the prominent individuals then before him their endowment. He needed no revelation, then, of a thing he had long experienced, any more than those now do, who have experienced the same things. It is only where experience fails, that revelation is needed. * * *

The Temple at Nauvoo passed into the hands of the enemy, who polluted it to that extent the Lord not only ceased to occupy it, but He loathed to have it called by His name, and permitted the wrath of its possessors to purify it by fire, as a token of what will speedily fall on them and their habitations, unless they repent.

But what are we here for, this day? To celebrate the birthday of our religion! To lay the foundation of a Temple to the Most High God, so that when His Son, our Elder Brother, shall again appear, he may have a place where he can lay his head, and not only spend a night or a day, but find a place of peace, that he may stay till he can say, "I am satisfied." (JD 2:31, 32, 33)

The Melchizedek Priesthood, which a woman shares in conjunction with her husband, is the authority by which the power of godliness is manifested. In preparation to receive the first endowment, this higher Priesthood is necessary:

And this greater priesthood administereth the gospel and holdeth the key of the mysteries of the kingdom, even the key of the knowledge of God. Therefore, in the ordinances thereof, the power of godliness is manifest.

And without the ordinances thereof, and the authority of the priesthood, the power of godliness is not manifest unto men in the flesh; for without this no man can see the face of God, even the Father, and live.

Now this Moses plainly taught to the children of Israel in the wilderness, and sought diligently to sanctify his people that they might behold the face of God;

But they hardened their hearts and could not endure his presence; therefore, the Lord in his wrath, for his anger was kindled against them, swore that they should not enter into his rest while in the wilderness, which rest is the fulness of his glory.

Therefore, he took Moses out of their midst, and the Holy Priesthood also; And the lesser priesthood continued, which priesthood holdeth the key of the ministering of angels and the preparatory gospel. (D & C 84:19-26)

The First Endowment

Among the most important instructions, commandments and ordinances taught to the early Church members by the Prophet Joseph Smith was the temple endowment:

The endowment you are so anxious about, you cannot comprehend now, nor could Gabriel explain it to the understanding of your dark minds; but strive to be prepared in your hearts, be faithful in all things, that when we meet in the solemn assembly, that is, when such as God shall name out of all the official members shall meet, we must be clean every whit. (TPJS, p. 91)

Nevertheless, an effort should be put forth to understand as clearly as possible the meaning and nature of the endowment—especially by those who wish to magnify their Priesthood. John A. Widtsoe explained:

> *The Temple endowment relates the story of man's eternal journey; sets forth the conditions upon which progress in the eternal journey depends; requires covenants or agreements of those participating, to accept and use the laws of progress; gives tests by which our willingness and fitness for righteousness may be known, and finally points out the ultimate destiny of those who love truth and live by it. (**Prst. & Ch. Gov.**, Widtsoe, p. 333)*

There are some who think that a woman receives the Priesthood when she gets her endowment. However, Heber C. Kimball clarified this:

> *Yes, it applies to you ladies, in your family capacity. You have not any priesthood, only in connection with your husbands. **You suppose that you receive the priesthood when you receive your endowments; but the priesthood is on your husbands.** (JD 5:31)*

This is also mentioned by Michael Homer, Salt Lake City attorney, in his Sunstone paper, presented in Salt Lake City, August 1994:

> *Even if Joseph Smith did not initially distinguish between "holding" and "sharing" the Priesthood, and some ambiguity was created when he and other Church leaders refer to the endowment as priesthood (perhaps because of its Masonic connection), Church leaders after the death of Joseph Smith have consistently taught that **women do not hold the Priesthood individually,** . . . ("Mormon Women and Sacred Ritual: From the Female Relief Society to the Holy Order")*

Even though the endowment is not an actual conferral of Priesthood, it does embrace the blessings, powers, privileges, and gifts from on High that pertain to that Priesthood.

Heber C. Kimball spoke to those who had received their first endowment:

> "You have been **anointed** to be kings and priests [or queens and priestesses], but you have not been **ordained to it yet**, and you have got to get it by being faithful." In the second anointing, the husband and wife are **ordained** "King and Queen, Priest and Priestess to the Most High God for time and throughout all eternity." (**Woman's Exponent** 13:61, Sept. 15, 1884)

Women, as well as men, can participate in both these privileges and blessings of the Priesthood.

When the Relief Society was about to be organized, the Prophet told the sisters, "I am glad to have the opportunity of organizing the women, as a part of the Priesthood belongs to them." And, "I will organize the sisters **under the priesthood after a pattern of the priesthood**." (Sarah S. Leavitt Autobiography, as quoted in **Mormon Enigma**, Newell & Avery, p. 106, and **Women's Voices**, Godfrey, et. al., see pp. 27-29.) He did NOT say "**with** the Priesthood" or "**in** the Priesthood", but "**under** the Priesthood" and "**after the pattern** of Priesthood".

> In 1906 Relief Society president Bathsheba Smith and secretary Emmeline Wells corrected a published historical account of the first Relief Society meeting that included Sarah M. Kimball's recollection that the Prophet had desired to organize women "in the order of the priesthood." Almost certainly at the request of the priesthood leaders concerned about misunderstanding, they searched for the phrase in the original Relief Society minutes and confirmed that "no such

statement was made" there. *("Relief Society Jubilee,"* **Woman's Exponent** *20:141, April 1, 1892)*

The Prophet indicated that both men and women are a **part of the organization** of Priesthood and that—

> . . . the **sisters would come in possession of the privileges, blessings, and gifts of the priesthood,** *and that signs should follow them. . . (DHC 4:602)*

This would include the privilege and blessings of the temple endowment.

Joseph Smith also gave another important message to the Relief Society in April of 1842:

> *He spoke of* **delivering the keys to this society and to the Church**—*that according to his prayers God had appointed him elsewhere. * * * That the keys of the kingdom are about to be given to them, that they may be able to detect everything false—as well as to the Elders.* **(Words of Joseph Smith,** *comp. by Ehat & Cook, p. 117)*

This same passage reads a little differently in the **DHC**:

> *He spoke of* **delivering the keys of the Priesthood to the Church,** *and said that the faithful members of the Relief Society should receive them in* **connection with their husbands,** *that the Saints whose integrity has been tried and proved faithful, might know* **how to ask the Lord and receive an answer;** *for according to his prayers, God had appointed him elsewhere. * * * for the keys of the kingdom are about to be given to them [Church leaders], that they may be able to detect everything false; . . . (DHC 4:604-05)*

This quote seems to be saying that with the Priesthood keys delivered to the Church, both men and women would then be able to learn the true order of prayer in order to receive answers to their prayers and "detect everything false."

It was shortly after this that Joseph transferred the "keys of the kingdom" from his shoulders to those of the Twelve with instructions that they should given them to others.

Some researchers feel that when Joseph Smith mentioned "delivering the keys to this society," in April 1842, he desired to give them Priesthood, but Michael Homer interestingly points out that this took place—

> . . . *before* the endowment had been given to the initial nine male members of the Holy Order and more than one and a half years before any women joined the order. *(In Sept. 1843 wives began to be endowed, anointed and sealed in plural marriage.) It is therefore more likely that the keys referred to the creation of a Society, which is the official interpretation, rather than Priesthood. . . . (1994 SLC Sunstone Symposium paper, op. cit.)*

On the 28th of May in 1843, Joseph Smith and Emma were "sealed" in marriage for time and eternity. This marriage ceremony consisted of promises and privileges pertaining to both mortality and eternity. In this ordinance Emma was promised that she could receive every blessing and promise that he should receive (based on her "faithfulness unto the end,") i.e., wherever he could go, she could go; there were no restrictions or qualifications because she did not have the Priesthood.

According to a statement by Pres. Wilford Woodruff, no man should administer in any of the ordinances in the temple without the Priesthood:

*Joseph Smith did not call upon any man to ordain or to baptize him, but he waited until the Lord sent forth His servants to administer unto him. He was commanded of the Lord to go forth and be baptized, but not until he had received the Priesthood. Where did he get it, and in fact what is the Priesthood? It is the authority of God in heaven to the **sons** of men to administer in any of the ordinances of His house. There never was a **man** and never will be a **man**, in this or any other age of the world, who has power and authority to administer in one of the ordinances of the house of God, unless **he** is called of God as was Aaron, unless **he** has the Holy Priesthood, and is administered to by those holding that authority.*

*There was no **man** on the face of the earth, nor had been for the last seventeen centuries, who had power and authority from God to go forth and administer in one of the ordinances of the house of God. (as quoted in **Prst. & Ch. Gov.**, Widtsoe, p. 27)*

And Widtsoe also explained:

*Ordinations of **men** to the Melchizedek Priesthood are performed as a necessary prerequisite to receiving the endowment of the Temple. (Ibid. p. 333)*

With women, however, it is a little different:

*It is a precept of the Church that women of the Church **share the authority of the Priesthood with their husbands**, actual or prospective; and therefore **women**, whether taking the endowment for themselves or for the dead, **are not ordained to specific rank in the Priesthood**. Nevertheless there is no grade, rank, or phase of the temple endowment to which women are not eligible on an equality with men. True, there are certain of the higher ordinances to which an unmarried woman cannot be admitted, but the rule is equally in force as to a bachelor. The married state is regarded as sacred, sanctified, and holy in all temple procedure; and within the House of the Lord the woman is the* *equal and the help-meet of the man. In the privileges and blessings of that holy place, the utterance of Paul is regarded as a scriptural decree in full force and effect: "Neither is the man without the woman, neither the woman without the man, in the Lord."* **(The House of the Lord***, Talmage, p. 94)*

The Priesthood is a power which extends beyond the grave, even being necessary to stand in the presence of God. Quoting again from Apostle Widtsoe:

Perhaps in no manner is the power of the Priesthood more evident than in the authority that it possesses to seal for time and eternity. For example, marriages may be consummated within the Church for all time—not merely until death doth them part. Family relationships may be continued throughout the eternities. **The power of the Priesthood extends beyond the grave.** *Temple work, including baptism, the endowment, sealing, etc., is a function of the Priesthood. It is by this power that work for the dead may be done. It is by the power of the Priesthood that a person may attain celestial glory. Without the* **power** *of the Priesthood one cannot enter the presence of God. (Prst. & Ch. Gov., p. 42)*

Thus, if a woman is to stand before God, then it is through this same **Priesthood power** that she is able to do so.

The First Endowment, then, shows men and women what they can achieve based upon their faithfulness and worthiness—a conditional promise that "they can become such". In the second anointing, the husband and wife (or wives) are actually ordained "king and queen, priest and priestess to the Most High God for time and throughout all eternity." **(Juve. Inst**. 15:111)

The Second Anointing

September 28, 1843 (exactly four months after their marriage had been sealed), Joseph and Emma Smith received their second anointing in an upper room of the Nauvoo Mansion House. They were the first couple in this dispensation to be "anointed and ordained to the highest and holiest order of the priesthood," also referred to as "the fullness of the Priesthood." (See "Joseph Smith's Introduction of Temple Ordinances. . .", Andrew Ehat, pp. 94-96.)

This higher ordinance was sometimes called a "second endowment," which is really not accurate because there is only one endowment for a person. Other terms are "highest ordinance" and "higher blessings," but the more proper term was given by Wilford Woodruff's First Presidency when people were writing to him to sign their temple recommend. They wrote: "This decision applies to all ordinances attended to in the House of the Lord, except **Second Anointings**, which last named will still require the approval of the President of the Church before they can be administered." (Mess. of the First Pres., Clark, 3:228)

It has been assumed by some that Priesthood was actually conferred upon women either in the first endowment or the second anointing. However, the wording in both of these ordinances makes no mention of conferring Priesthood through those administrations.

Prior to the actual second anointing ceremony, there should be the ordinance of washing of feet:

_____, *having authority of Jesus Christ, I wash your right foot that you may forever step forward in the cause of truth and righteousness and your left foot that you may forever stand fast in defense of the faith*

*and testimony of Jesus. . . . ("Second Anointings, A Brief
Look at a Little Known Ordinance," by Lisle G. Brown)*

Then when the brethren receive their second anointings, there is an advancement to a higher Priesthood
office or title—a King and a Priest unto God. With this
anointing, however, there is no more or new Priesthood
conferred on them. The wording in the second anointing—as it was given in the Nauvoo Temple to some of the
Twelve Apostles by Brigham Young—is included in the
following reference:

*Pres. Brigham Young proceeded to anoint Br. Heber C.
Kimball and Vilate his wife—and pronounced the following blessings namely, "Bro. Heber Chase Kimball, in the
name of Jesus Christ we pour upon thy head this holy
oil and we anoint thee a King and a Priest unto the Most
High God, in and over the Church of Jesus Christ of
Latter Day Saints and also Israel in this the Holy Temple
of the Lord at Nauvoo, the City of Joseph, state of
Illinois. . . ." ("Book of Anointings," p. 3, Church
Historians's Office Library; remainder of ordinance
wording is in the possession of the author, describing
the anointing of his head, ears, eyes, and mouth)*

*He then anointed Sister Vilate Kimball a Queen and
Priestess unto her husband (H.C. Kimball) in the Church
of Jesus Christ of Latter Day Saints and in Israel, and
pronounced all the blessings upon her head in common
with her husband. (**Ibid.**, p. 4))*

When Heber C. Kimball anointed Brigham Young for
his second anointing, these words were used:

*Brother Brigham Young, I pour this holy, consecrated oil,
upon your head, and anoint thee a King and a Priest of the
Most High God over the Church of Jesus Christ of Latter
Day Saints, and unto all Israel. [He then proceeded in the*

*anointing of the various parts of the body, etc.) For there shall be given unto thee crowns, and kingdoms, and dominions; . . . (**Ibid.**, p. 2)*

President Kimball then anointed Mary Ann Young, wife of Brigham Young:

*Sister Mary Ann Young, I pour upon thy head this holy, consecrated oil, and seal upon thee all the **blessings** of the everlasting priesthood, **in conjunction with thy husband:** and I anoint thee to be a Queen and Priestess unto thy husband, over the Church of Jesus Christ of Latter Day Saints; and thou shalt be heir to all the blessings which are sealed upon him, inasmuch as **thou dost obey his counsel**; and thou shalt receive glory, honor, power and exaltation in his exaltation; and thou shalt be a strength in thy mind for thou shalt have visions, and manifestations of the Holy Spirit, and the time shall come that angels shall visit thee, and minister unto thee, and teach thee; and in the absence of thy husband shall comfort thee, and make known his situation.*
* * *

*And I seal thee up unto Eternal Life; thou shalt come forth in the morning of the first resurrection and inherit with him all the honors, glories, and power of Eternal Lives, and that thou shalt attain unto the eternal Godhead, so thy exaltation shall be perfect, and thy glory be full, in a fulness of power and exaltation. (**Ibid.**, pp. 4-5)*

There are a few points in the above ceremony that need to be emphasized:

1. The **blessings** of the Priesthood were sealed upon her—not the   Priesthood itself.

2. These blessings were sealed in **conjunction with her husband.**

3. She was anointed to be a Queen and Priestess **unto her husband.**

4. She would be heir to the same blessings that were sealed **upon her husband**.

5. She was still instructed to **obey her husband's counsel.**

6. She would receive "glory, honor, power and exaltation **in his exaltation.**"

7. No Priesthood was actually **conferred** upon her.

It is once again evident that even after receiving the Second Anointing, the woman holds the Priesthood only in conjunction with her husband, and enjoys the benefits of its blessings and powers through him.

As in every kingly status, the king still presides over the queen. An anointed king in the Priesthood is the supreme head, the governor or president over that house or kingdom, yet the queen shares in all he possesses, both temporal and spiritual.

This established order continues to exist even outside the eternal family unit, for Isaiah stated:

> And kings shall be thy nursing fathers, and their queens thy nursing mothers: they shall bow down to thee with their face toward the earth, and lick up the dust of thy feet, and thou shalt know that I am the Lord. . . . (Isa. 49:23)

Why would kings and queens bow down to someone else? Simply because of a higher authority—a greater king and queen than those of an earthly calling.

The disciples of Jesus admitted this, for John wrote that Jesus "hast made us unto our God kings and priests: and we shall reign on the earth." (Rev. 5:10) John called Him the "King of kings" (17:14). He is the King of other kings which he so ordained as His kings and their queens.

It was written in the law of the Lord on high, that they that overcome by obedience, should be made kings and queens, and priests and priestesses to God and his Father, through the atonement of the eldest son, and that natural eyes should not see, nor natural ears hear, neither should the natural heart conceive the great, glorious, and eternal things, honors and blessings, that were then, in the Father's dominions, and mansions, prepared in the beginning for them that kept the faith to the end, and entered triumphantly into their third estates: (the eternal life). (**T & S** *6:917*)

The receiving of this second anointing should be a primary objective of all righteous men and women who call themselves Saints. Charles W. Penrose admonished:

We should be a nation of kings and priests unto God, a royal priesthood, a peculiar people zealous of good works. This is what we should be, my brethren and sisters. (JD 20:127)

These were blessings and promises which have rarely been on the earth; and when they have been here, most of the people were unworthy of them. As George Q. Cannon stated:

But God designed when He led Israel out of Egypt to make of that people a royal Priesthood—a kingdom of Kings and Priests. He designed to lead them forward under the guidance of the everlasting Priesthood, the Priesthood after the holy order of the Son of God—to lead them forward until they should behold the face of their God and see Him for themselves. But they would not. They hardened their hearts. They could not endure His presence. (JD 25:290)

As mentioned, in this ordinance of the Second Anointing, the couple are anointed as a "King and Queen, Priest and Priestess to the Most High God for time and throughout all eternity." (**Juve. Instr**. 15:111)

> *In the Mormon temple, woman is not merely implied, but well defined and named. There the theme of the song of the New Jerusalem is faithfully rendered in her personality. If man is anointed priest unto God, woman is anointed priestess; if symboled in his heavenly estate as king, she is also symboled as queen. (**Women of Mormondom**, Tullidge, p. 488)*

The Prophet Joseph attempted to prepare and elevate Church members to the point of receiving these higher blessings—the fullness of the Priesthood. This royal Priesthood order of kings and queens was to be part of the kingdom which would last forever. The Prophet Joseph said:

> *Those holding the fullness of the Melchizedek Priesthood are kings and priests of the Most High God, holding the keys of power and blessings. In fact, that Priesthood is a perfect law of theocracy, and stands as God to give laws to the people, administering endless lives to the sons and daughters of Adam. (TPJS, p. 322)*

And again—

> *The Prophet taught further that through the rites of the temple, faithful women would achieve **exaltation** within the eternal family order, as **priestesses and as queens to their husbands and over their posterity for endless ages of time.** This meant that within the home, women shared **priesthood rights** with their husbands. **A priestess is a female priest—one who exercises priestly rights and powers by virtue of the priesthood.** In this context, a queen is a woman with a political stature and*

*power in the home, **within the patriarchal order of the priesthood**. * * **

*The priesthood **rights** of women pertained to the home; they did not extend in a general way to the Church, but within the divine patriarchal order, a woman's ministry in the home was derived from the priesthood, and the functions of teaching, guiding, and directing her family were priestly acts. (**Doc. of the Kingdom**, Hyrum Andrus, pp. 411-412)*

It has never been the policy of the LDS Church to allow a woman to receive her Second Anointing except with her husband. It would even be less probable to allow a single woman to ever receive those blessings. This subject was taken up by the First Presidency in a letter dated November 1904:

Nov. 4, 1904

Prest. Thomas R. Bassett
Rexburg, Idaho

Dear Brother:

*Referring to yours of the 1st inst., recommending Sister Harriot B. Rowberry for second anointing, we would say that **a woman cannot receive those blessings except in connection with her husband;** and a man so indifferent to the ordinances of the house of the Lord as to neglect doing his own temple work in his lifetime, although, as you say, he might have done so had he been so inclined, can scarcely be considered worthy of second anointing, and we do not see how you can consistently recommend him to receive those blessings.*

For these reasons we have withheld your endorsement from the recommend sent by you in favor of Sister Rowberry.

Your Brethrenn
(s) Joseph F. Smith
(s) John R. Winder
(s) Anthon H. Lund

(Historical Dept., "Confidential Research Files, 1950-1974," LDS Church Archives, Jan. 10, 1905)

The rules for a man and a woman to receive their second anointings were generally the same—they would both receive them together. James E. Talmage wrote, "True, there are certain of the higher ordinances to which an unmarried woman cannot be admitted, but the rule is equally in force as to a bachelor." (**The House of the Lord**, p. 94)

However, there have been a few exceptions to this rule, as Michael Quinn researched:

This requires acknowledgement that Wilford Woodruff's diary says the following men received the second anointing alone, since their wives had not yet been endowed and were not present: Parley P. Pratt on 21 January 1844, Orson Hyde on 25 January 1844, Orson Pratt on 26 January 1844, and William Clayton on 3 February 1844. Joseph Smith's diaries indicate the same thing. The reference to Clayton is incorrect and arose from his name having appeared immediately after the second anointing for Joseph and Clarissa Young. Clayton's diary shows that he received only the first anointing in 1844, and Heber C. Kimball's diary in December 1845 listed Clayton among the Anointed Quorum's members who had not yet received "their Last [or second] Anointing." However, there is no mistake in the "second anointing" reference to the Pratt brothers and Orson Hyde. (Quinn, op. cit., p. 397, ftnt. 35)

It is rather difficult for a man to be a king, presiding over a kingdom, without a queen. That is the established structure and order that also pertains to the Holy Priesthood.

The following sample quotations illustrate five different cases of couples getting their second anointings. These were quite common in the early years of the Church, but in this part of the 20th century, they are enjoyed only by some of the Church hierarchy.

The summer of 1845 I spent a portion of the time labor-ing on the [Nauvoo] Temple and a portion for the support of my family. On the 23rd of December myself and wife Elizabeth received our washing and anointing in the temple, and on the 19th of January, 1846, we were sealed, agreeable to the order of the Holy Priesthood, for time and for all eternity. On the 22nd of January we received our **second anointing,** *on which day my father and mother also received theirs. (***Wm. Hyde Autobiography***, BYU Library, p. 16)*

In the fall of 1845 I was again taken sick with chills and fever, and was unable to do a day's work for eight months. During this time in the winter of 1845 and 1846, notwithstanding my sickness, I went into the tem-ple in Nauvoo and received my endowments by washing and anointing and was sealed to my wife Sophia for time and all eternity, and afterwards we were anointed the **second time a king and queen** *in the kingdom of God. (***Noah Packard Autobiography***, typescript, BYU-S Library, p. 9)*

January 11, 1846. I was called on to go to work in the [Nauvoo] Temple which I did. I assisted in the forenoon, afternoon and at night I anointed some 70 persons. Twenty-six of us were called upon to go to the temple and be sealed to Brother Heber C. Kimball. The next Friday we were invited to go to Father Kimball's and we received some good instructions and enjoyed ourselves in a dance, also.

The next week we were to work in the temple and father Kimball called on me to go home and get my wife and also James Smith and wife to be sealed to our wives. We did this. We were conducted into another department and received our **Second Anointing.** *This was a source of knowledge to us and it was a great con-solation that we were counted worthy before our Father in Heaven to receive that which we did receive. (***Joseph Hovey Autobiography***, BYU Library, p. 34)*

Apostate spirits within were now joining with our ene-mies outside for the destruction of the priesthood, for the

Temple was progressing, and the devil, striving for empire, began to stir up, in them as in Judas, desire for the Prophet's blood. The keys of endowments and plural marriage had been given, and some had received their **Second Anointing**. *(Benjamin Johnson,* **My Life's Review**, *1847, p. 98)*

June 22, 1870. Myself with my three wives Susan, Janet, and Margaret and my son James with two teams all started for Salt Lake City and arrived at the city on the second day of July. On the sixth day Susan and myself with my sister Esther M. Lebaron went to the Endowment House and were baptized and sealed for the following persons. (Names listed) Esther was also baptized for Julia and Survina Taft, both my cousins, and were both sealed to me. My wife Susan was baptized and sealed for Charlotte Fuller, Darney Lyman, Harriet Webster and Lucy Holms, all sealed to me.

July 7th, 1870. Myself and three wives all went to the Endowment House and received our **second anointing** *under the hand of President Daniel H. Wells. (**Joel Johnson Autobiography**, BYU Collection)*

After the turn of the century, the second anointings started to gradually fade out, and during the presidency of Heber J. Grant there were years in which no second anointings were recorded.

So, instead of being a "nation of kings and queens," very few of the nine million members of the Church today have received these ordinations. Is it because not many Latter-day Saints are worthy of these highest ordinations? Has the Church hierarchy just kept these sacred ordinances for themselves? Or have they lost the calling and authority to even perform such anointings? Either we are no better than the ancient Israelites who had the higher priesthood taken out of their midst, or many worthy members are being deprived of their proper blessings.

Even in 1854 John Taylor pled with the Saints:

Well, what is it we are engaged in? Is the object of our being, in this life, attained by thinking of nothing else but horses, to look to nothing else but our little interests, our little farm or house, a few cattle, and the like? Is this all we are concerned in, ye Latter-day Saints? And if some of these things do not come smooth and square according to your notions; and if you have made your golden or some other darling idol, and a Moses should come along and break it to pieces and stamp it under his feet, and scatter it abroad, and say, "Arise, Israel, and wake from your slumbers;" do you feel very much grieved? Do you feel as though some dreadful calamity had happened to you? Have you forgot who you are, and what your object is? Have you forgot that you profess to be Saints of the Most High God, clothed upon with the Holy Priesthood? **Have you forgot that you are aiming to become Kings and Priests to the Lord, and Queens and Priestesses to Him?** *(JD 1:372-373)*

And a few years later, in 1857 and 1858, Elder Taylor again reminded the Saints:

What are we engaged in? We are engaged in building up the kingdom of God, and many of you have been ordained by the revelations of the Almighty to hold the power and authority of the Holy Priesthood. Besides this, you have been ordained **kings and queens**, *and* **priests and priestesses** *to your Lord; you have been put in possession of principles that all the kings, potentates, and powers upon the earth are entirely ignorant of; they do not understand it; but you have received this from the hands of God. (JD 5:190)*

We are all aiming at celestial glory. Don't you know we are? We are talking about it, and we talk about being **kings and priests** *unto the Lord; we talk about being enthroned in the kingdoms of our God; we talk about being* **queens and priestesses**; *and we talk,*

when we get on our high-heeled shoes, about possess-
ing thrones, principalities, power, and dominions in the
eternal worlds, when at the same time many of us do
not know how to conduct ourselves any better than a
donkey does. (JD 6:166)

Apostle John Taylor's advice is just as appropriate for us today and particularly applies to those men and women who are continually clamoring for women to be ordained to the priesthood. Righteous LDS endowed and married women already have all the powers and bless-ings of Priesthood that they need. The problem is they don't recognize and magnify what they have. Margaret Toscano, in her article entitled, "If Mormon Women Have Had the Priesthood Since 1843, Why Aren't They Using It?", answers her own question:

Why aren't women using their priesthood? Because
they are prevented from doing so by the current policy of
the church which many assume to be the will of God
without examining the historical evidence or theological
assumptions behind this policy. * * * While women do
not need and should not ask permission from male lead-
ers to use their priesthood in private ways or accepted
venues, it is impossible for them to use it in visible ways
or in official capacities without an acknowledgement of
*women's right to priesthood. (**Dialogue** 27:2, Summer*
1994, p. 224, 223)

George Q. Cannon realized the potential of worthy brothers and sisters in the Gospel:

The genius of the kingdom with which we are associ-
ated is to disseminate knowledge through all the ranks
of the people, and to make every man a prophet and
*every **woman a prophetess,** that they may understand*
the plans and purposes of God. (JD 12:46)

In our day the term "queen" is tossed around until we have lost the real scope and intent of a true queen. We now have beauty queens, international queens, carnival queens, cotton queens, milk queens, drag queens, queen bees, and even queen for a day. Those we seem to understand and value, but we've lost sight of God's queens.

The questions then arise—after being anointed a king and a queen, what are their additional responsibilities and callings? Are these just honorary titles, or are they actual offices with specific duties associated thereto?

When Heber C. Kimball gave Brigham Young his second anointing, he promised him—

> . . . thou mayest be enabled to speak the great things of God, and confound all the wisdom of man, and put to nought all who shall raise up to oppose thee, in all countries where thou goest for thou shalt build up the Kingdom of God among many people, and in the midst of mighty nations; so thy glory shall be established, and whosoever thou shalt bind on earth, shall be bound in heaven, and whomsoever thou shalt loose on earth, shall be loosed in heaven; for there shalt be given unto thee crowns, and kingdoms, and dominions; . . . ("Book of Anointings", p. 2-3)

Orson Pratt described the tremendous power of the Priesthood of God, and distinguishes between **kingly** and **priestly** authority:

> The Priesthood of God is the great, supreme, legal authority that governs the inhabitants of all redeemed and glorified worlds. In it is included all power to create worlds, to ordain fixed and permanent laws for the regulation of the materials in all their varied operations, whether acting as particles, as masses, as worlds, or as clusters of worlds. It is that power that formed the minerals, the vegetables, and the animals in all their infinite varieties which exist upon our globe.

It is that authority that reveals laws for the government of intelligent beings—that rewards the obedient and punishes the disobedient—that ordains principalities, powers, and kingdoms to carry out its righteous administrations throughout all dominions. The **Kingly** *authority is not separate and distinct from the Priesthood, but merely a* **branch or portion of the same.** *The* **Priestly** *authority is universal, having power over all things; the* **Kingly** *authority until perfected is limited to the kingdoms placed under its jurisdiction: the former appoints and ordains the latter; but the latter never appoints and ordains the former: the first controls the laws of nature, and exercises jurisdiction over the elements, as well as over men; the last controls men only, and administers just and righteous laws for their government. Where the two are combined and the individual perfected, he has almighty power both as a King and as a Priest; both offices are then merged in one. The distinctions then, will be merely in the name and not in the authority:* **either as a King or a Priest he will then have power and dominion over all things**, *and reign over all. Both titles, combined, will then not give him any more power than either one singly. It is evident that the distinctions of title are only expressive of the condition of things prior to the glorification and perfection of the persons who hold the Priesthood; for when they are perfected, they will have power to act in every branch of authority by virtue of the great, and almighty, and eternal Priesthood which they hold: they can then sway their sceptres as Kings; rule as Princes, minister as Apostles; officiate as Teachers; or, act in the humblest or most exalted capacity. There is no branch of the Priesthood so low that they cannot condescend to officiate therein; none so high, that they cannot reach forth the arm of power and control the same. (**The Seer,** Pratt, vol. 1, No. 10, p. 145)*

As Queen, of course, the wife is by her King's side—sharing in all these responsibilities, callings and powers.

In the English definition, **queen** is one who "reigns in her own right" and is the wife of the reigning monarch. Among the Jews some of the queens received a special recognition and honor. The Queen of Sheba was the first woman to receive that title in Bible history. She gives us much reason to respect such qualities in all women. As Herbert Lockyer wrote:

> [The] Queen of Sheba was of the Semitic race and not wholly alien from the stock of Abraham. Queens were not unusual in her region (Acts 8:27). Legend has it that she was a ruler of the great kingdom of South Arabia and that she was renowned for her beauty, wealth and magnificence.
>
> Through commercial intercourse the queen came to learn of the wisdom and wealth of Solomon and was determined to find out for herself the truth of all she had heard. * * *
>
> The queen came to Solomon, we are told, to ask him "concerning the name of the Lord" and to "prove him with hard questions." Such was no idle curiosity, which can be a good master as well as a bad one. In the queenÕs case, curiosity was the stepping stone to revelation and higher wisdom. She undertook a long journey, for those times, and at fabulous cost, to sit before Solomon and learn of his wisdom. She felt that no effort was too great or price too high for an introduction to the king's superb wisdom. She did not come on a visit of state or to enter into some kind of treaty, or even to behold Solomon's magnificence. Her quest was for wisdom and for a fuller knowledge of Solomon's God. (See Isaiah 60:3, 6, 19, 20)
>
> With all the pomp and pageantry, culture and commerce the queenÕs country represented, she had no need to curry even Solomon's favor. She sought the widening of her mental and spiritual horizon. ***
>
> Does not this queen represent those young women of today with a thirst for higher knowledge and culture, all that is artistically beautiful, and for the poetry of religion? Receptive to wisdom, they become wise. Their lives are enriched by contact with intellectual superiori-

ty, reading and questioning. **Would that more could be found following the Queen of Sheba in her quest! (All the Kings and Queens of the Bible,** *Lockyer, Zondervan Publishing, pp. 211, 212, 213)*

Today we seem to have lost sight of the most important blessings that God has prepared for His people. We are immersed in the temporal jungles of Babylon, searching for ridiculous honors and titles among the gentiles instead of those esteemed offices and callings of the Priesthood. We want the honors of prominent men in the business world instead of kings and queens in the Kingdom of God. Our failure with the Priesthood and its higher ordinations is even greater than that of ancient Israel.

"Looking to the fruition of the divine program in eternity, Brigham Young promised" (Doc. of the Kingdom, Andrus, p. 411):

Now, brethren, the man that honors his Priesthood, the woman that honors her Priesthood, will receive an everlasting inheritance in the kingdom of God; *but it will not be until this earth is purified and sanctified, and ready to be offered up to the Father. But we can go to work now and live as near as we can like the family of heaven, that we may secure to ourselves the blessings of heaven and of earth, of time and of eternity, and life everlasting in the presence of the Father and the Son. This is what we want to do. Remember it, brethren and sisters, and try to live worthy of the vocation of your high calling. You are called to be Saints—just think of and realize it, for the greatest honor and privilege that can be conferred upon a human being is to have the privilege of being a Saint. The honor of the kings and queens of the earth fades into insignificance when compared with the title of a Saint. You may possess earthly power, and rule with an iron hand, but that power is nothing, it will soon be broken and pass away;*

but the power of those who live and honor the Priesthood will increase forever and ever. (JD 17:119-120)

* * *

The endowment, then, is a passport to "enable you to walk back into the presence of the Father" (B.Y.) by the use of certain keys, signs and tokens. The blessings and promises of both the first endowment and the second anointing are available for both worthy men and women alike.

Chapter 9

"THEY SHALL BE ONE FLESH"

Vocal music reaches its greatest power and beauty in the harmonious blending of more than one voice. The energy, power and usefulness of electricity results from the combination of both the negative and the positive wires. Scissors are useless without both halves. So must men and women be spiritually united to receive the fullness of Priesthood blessings and promises.

The instruction to "be one flesh" was given to mankind at the beginning of this world:

> *And Adam said, This I know now is bone of my bones, and flesh of my flesh. She shall be called woman, because she was taken out of man. Therefore shall a man leave his father and mother, and shall cleave unto his wife; and **they shall be one flesh**. (Gen. 2:29-30, I.V.)*

It should be understood that being one in flesh has to do with the physical union—and does not mean necessarily one in spirit, purpose or principle, although that is certainly the ideal. Paul explained to the Corinthians:

> *Know ye not that your bodies are the members of Christ? Shall I then take the members of Christ, and make them the members of an harlot? God forbid.*

> *What? know ye not that he which is joined to an har-*
> *lot is one body? for two, saith he, shall be one flesh.*
> *But he that is joined unto the Lord is one spirit. (I Cor.*
> *6:15-17)*

When a woman is sealed to a man by Priesthood authority, she should then become one with him in every aspect: not just physically, but spiritually, emotionally, intellectually, etc. She then shares his life, his name, his glory, and **his Priesthood.**

Birthright to the Priesthood

Neither man nor woman is born with the Priesthood, although they can come into mortality with the **right** to it or as **heirs** to it, because of lineage:

> *What is meant by the command in Isaiah, 52d chap-*
> *ter, 1st verse, which saith: Put on thy strength, O Zion—*
> *and what people had Isaiah reference to?*
> *He had reference to those whom God should call in the*
> *last days, who should hold the power of priesthood to*
> *bring again Zion, and the redemption of Israel; and to*
> *put on her strength is to **put on the authority of the***
> ***priesthood, which she, Zion, has a right to by line-***
> ***age**; . . . (D & C 113:7-8)*

The birthright to the Priesthood, however, is not the Priesthood itself, but a **right** to have it. Abraham learned that he was of the lineage which had the right to the Priesthood and went to Melchizedek telling him of that birthright; thereupon Melchizedek conferred the Priesthood upon Abraham; and when he left, he said, "Now I have a priesthood." (TPJS, p. 323; DHC 5:555)

Michael Quinn explains this further:

*In February 1844 stake patriarch John Smith told an LDS woman that she had a **right to priesthood from her birth.** "Thou art of the blood of Abraham thru the loins of Manasseh and **lawful heir to the Priesthood,"** he said to Louisa C. Jackson. She was not among the elite Mormon women who received the endowment before the opening of the Nauvoo Temple in December 1845. Referring to her eventual sealing and second anointing, the patriarch added that this woman "shall possess it [priesthood] **in common with thy companion."** Louisa's blessing showed that any Mormon woman had a birthright to priesthood which depended on no man. (John Smith's patriarchal blessing, Feb. 6, 1844, RLDS Archives, as quoted in Quinn's article in Women and Authority, p. 369)*

This passage, along with Doctrine and Covenants 113, shows us that the right to enjoy the "authority of the Priesthood" is passed down through those men and women who are of the chosen lineage.

In Connection with Their Husbands

Throughout the writings of Mormonism we find the message reiterated that **women share the Priesthood with their husbands**. This was reinforced as the official Church position by John Taylor in 1880, as described and verified by Linda Newell in her article "The Historical Relationship of Mormon Women and Priesthood:"

Sarah Granger Kimball, whose idea it was to organize the women of Nauvoo, had used the priesthood structure as a pattern for the Relief Society in her ward, complete with deaconesses and teachers. (Sarah M. Kimball, 15th Ward R.S. Minutes, 1868, LDS Archives) However, John Taylor, who had originally ordained those first officers in March 1842, explained that "some of the sisters have thought that these sisters mentioned were, in this ordination, ordained to the priesthood . . . [but] **it is not the calling of these sisters to hold the Priesthood, only in connection with their husbands,** *they being one with their husbands. (JD 21:367-68) This 1880 statement has stood as the official interpretation. (Newell, as quoted in Women and Authority, Hanks, p. 29)*

The following several references—samples from 1842 to 1896—give further support to this position:

1842

*On the occasion of the organization of the Relief Society (April 1842), by the Prophet Joseph Smith at Nauvoo, I (John Taylor) was present. Sister Emma Smith was elected president and Sisters Elizabeth Ann Whitney and Sarah M. Cleveland her counselors. * * * The ordination then given did not mean the conferring of the Priesthood upon those sisters, yet the sisters hold a portion of the Priesthood* **in connection with their husbands.** *(Sisters Eliza R. Snow and Bathsheba W. Smith stated that they so understood it in Nauvoo and have looked upon it always in that light.) (**The Woman's Exponent** 9:53, Sept. 1, 1880)*

1844

You shall be blessed in **common with your husband, and shall receive all the blessings of the Priesthood that are sealed upon his head,** *even the seal of the covenant. (Hyrum Smith's Patriarchal Blessing to Sarah Forstner Zundel, Jan. 31, 1844, "Record of the Ancestry and Descendants of John Jacob Zundel", p. 63, LDS Church Library)*

1845

The Father commissioned him to preach the gospel to them and show them the plan by which they could be brought up in the resurrection and prepare themselves for higher glories. This is the way that he spent the time, and this is the way that every person who holds the priesthood will spend the time that intervenes between his death and his resurrection. The spirits of men are not all that will be employed in this delightful task; but you, too, my sisters, will take a part therein, for **you will hold a portion of the priesthood with your husbands,** *and you will thus do a work, as well as they, that will augment that glory which you will enjoy after your resurrection. (Orson Pratt, at the funeral of Mrs. Caroline Smith, June 1, 1845,* **T & S** *6:920)*

Sister[s] . . . have no right to meddle in the affairs of the kingdom of God . . . [they] never can hold the Priesthood apart from their husbands. (Brigham Young, **Seventies Record***, Mar. 9, 1845)*

1846

Here is a blessing given by Patriarch John Smith to Emily Jacob in 1846: "I place my hands upon thy head in the name of Jesus of Nazareth and **seal upon thee the Priesthood** *with all the blessings of the new and everlasting covenant, which was sealed upon the children of Joseph, for this [is] thy lineage, the same as thy companion.* **Thou hast a right to all the blessings which are sealed upon his head, for a woman can have but little power in the priesthood without a man.***" (City of Joseph, the Record of Norton Jacob, pp. 16-17; Jan. 26, 1846)*

1856

I accordingly asked Mr. [Heber C.] Kimball if women had a right to wash and anoint the sick for the recovery of their health or is it mockery in them to do so? He replied inasmuch as they are obedient to their husbands, they have a right to administer in that way in the name of the Lord Jesus Christ but **not by authority of the priesthood invested in them for that authority is not given to woman***. He also said they might administer* **by the authority given to their husbands** *inasmuch as they were one with their husbands. (Mary Ellen Abel Kimball Diary, 2 Mar. 1856, LDS archives)*

In another blessing given by Elisha Graves to Lucy Flake, again the necessity of holding the priesthood in order to do temple work is indicated: "thou art a royal heir to all the blessings, privileges and powers which pertain to the Holy Priesthood according to thy sex, which thou shalt receive in due time that thou mayest be able to accomplish thy work in behalf of thy progenitors. Thou shalt be connected with **a man of God, thru whom thou shalt receive the priesthood,** exaltation, power and eternal glory, become a mother in Israel. . . . be anointed a queen and priestess unto the most high God, receive thy crown, dominion, power and eternal increase, thy inheritance with thy benefactor in Zion." *("Life of Lucy Hannah White Flake," pp. 4-5; blessing given by Elisha H. Graves, Nov. 4th, 1856)*

1857

Tell about loving God and His people! If you do not love the man that leads you, you do not love that Being who confers all the blessings and privileges we enjoy. Tell about loving God, and not love the men that lead you! Get out with your nonsense. Will that apply to the Elders? Yes, and to the Seventies, the High Priests, Bishops, Teachers, and all men. Any further? Yes, it applies to you ladies, in your family capacity. **You have not any priesthood, only in connection with your husbands. You suppose that you receive the priesthood when you receive your endowments; but the priesthood is on your husbands.** *Can you honour God and the Priesthood, and abuse your husbands like the Devil? How can you honour the Priesthood, except you honour the man you are connected with? (Heber C. Kimball, JD 5:31, July 12, 1857)*

Some of you ladies, that go abroad from house to house, blessing the sick, having your little circles of women come together, why are you troubling your-selves to bless and lay your hands on women, and prophesy on them, if you do not believe the principle? You make yourselves fools to say that that same power should not be on the man that has got the Priesthood, and **with sisters that have not got any, only what they hold in connection with their husbands.** *(Heber C. Kimball, JD 5:177, Aug. 23, 1857)*

I do not care so much about the women obeying as I do the men. I am not talking about them, but you, Elders of Israel, that have the Priesthood. **Women have not a particle of Priesthood, only what they hold in connection with their husbands;** *neither have the men, except that which they hold in connection with those who hold the keys of the kingdom at headquarters. (Heber C. Kimball, JD 6:67, Nov. 22, 1857)*

1879

Our sisters are engaged with us in trying to do a good work. Shall we despise them in their labors? No. Who are they? Part of ourselves. Do they hold the priesthood? **Yes, in connection with their husbands** *and they are one with their husbands, but the husband is the head. (John Taylor, JD 20:359, Nov. 30, 1879)*

1880

At that meeting the Prophet called Sister Emma to be an elect lady. That means that she was called to a certain work; and that was in fulfillment of a certain revelation concerning her. She was elected to preside over the Relief Society, and she was ordained to expound the Scriptures. In compliance with Brother Joseph's request, I set her apart, and also ordained Sister Whitney, wife of Bishop Newel K. Whitney, and Sister Cleveland, wife of Judge Cleveland, to be her counselors.

Some of the sisters have thought that these sisters mentioned were, in this ordination, ordained to the priesthood. And for the information of all interested in this subject I will say, **it is not the calling of these sisters to hold the Priesthood, only in connection with their husbands,** *they being one with their husbands. (John Taylor, JD 21:367-68)*

1887

*The father of a family is the patriarch; he holds in his hands the keys of blessing for every member of his family, and is their head. His wives, be they few or many, are given to him (and here it is that the man is not without the woman), that through them he may not only perpetuate his name and continue his generation, but that through them the Priesthood may be continued also; for sorrowful indeed is the condition of that family which is without a man holding the Priesthood to stand before the Lord in their behalf. As we have said, while the man holds the keys independently, what power his wives have is in him and not in themselves alone. Let us illustrate. The Revelator John talks of our becoming Kings and Priests. When this time arrives, a man then becomes a King and a Priest to God; but a woman becomes a Queen and Priestess to her husband. And though a man may have a thousand, yet each woman holds this right independent of any other woman, when the blessing is conferred upon her; but **no woman can receive this blessing unless she is allied to a man who has attained to this power.** We repeat, the man can receive this blessing also independently; whereas **the woman receives it because of and through her husband.***

Her glory, her exaltation, and all the blessings pertaining to eternal lives will also come through this channel. But as woman, through the power of the gospel, can rise above that part of the curse pertaining to her fallen state which says, "Thy desire shall be to thy husband," so will she gradually merge into that more pleasing condition which will bring to her a fulness of joy for evermore; **possessing, as she will, all that power, authority and rule that belongs to her in connection with, and not separate from her husband.** *(Joseph E. Taylor, Des. Evng. News, Dec. 24, 1887)*

1888

Now, I ask you: Is it possible that we have the holy priesthood and our wives have none of it? Do you not see, by what I have read, that **Joseph desired to** *confer these keys of power upon them in connection with their husbands? I hold that a faithful wife has certain* **blessings, powers and rights**, *and is made partaker of certain* **gifts and blessings and promises with her husband**, *which she cannot be deprived of, except by transgression of the holy order of God. (Franklin D. Richards, Coll. Dis. 5:19, July 19, 1888)*

1896

In 1889 a monthly magazine for women was published for the Young Ladies Mutual Improvement Association. It was established by Brigham Young's daughter, Susa Young Gates, and in 1896 an article appeared saying that—

". . . the Seventy's wife bears the priesthood of the Seventy **in connection with her husband**, *and shares in its responsibilities." (**Young Women's Jrnl.** 7:398)*

Church Position Changes

Around the turn of the century, this understanding of women holding Priesthood in connection with their husbands began to fade away, along with many other doctrines. Note the contradiction made by Joseph F. Smith in 1907:

Does a wife hold the priesthood with her husband, and may she lay hands on the sick with him, with authority? **A wife does** <u>not</u> **hold the priesthood with her husband, but she enjoys the benefits thereof with him;** *and if she is requested to lay hands on the sick with him, or with any other officer holding the Melchizedek Priesthood, she may do so with perfect propriety. It is no uncommon thing for a man and wife unitedly to administer to their children. (**Doc. of Sal.** 3:122; Era 10:308)*

Also in 1907, over the signatures of Joseph F. Smith and his two counselors, an "Address to the World" was publicized wherein it clearly stated:

> We affirm that through the ministration of immortal personages, the Holy Priesthood has been conferred upon **men** in the present age, and that under this divine authority, the Church of Christ has been organized. (**Mess. of First Pres**. 4:144-45)

However, it is interesting to note that John A. Widtsoe was still teaching in 1915:

> **Women enjoy all the endowments and blessings of the Priesthood in connection with their husbands**. The family is the basis of society on earth, and as there must be organization among intelligent beings, someone must be spokesman for the family. In the family, the man is the spokesman and presiding authority, and, therefore, the Priesthood is bestowed upon him. (Rational Theology, Widtsoe, 1st ed. 1915, p. 97)

But in 1921 Charles W. Penrose of the First Presidency stated:

> Sisters have said to me sometimes, "But, I hold the Priesthood with my husband." "Well," I asked, "what office do you hold in the Priesthood?" Then they could not say much more. **The sisters are not ordained to any office in the Priesthood and there is authority in the Church which they cannot exercise**: it does not belong to them; they cannot do that properly any more than they can change themselves into a man. (Conf. Rept., Apr. 1921, p. 198)

And the same General Conference, Rudger Clawson explained:

The Priesthood is not received, or held or exer-
cised in any degree, by the women of the church;
but, nevertheless, the women of the church enjoy the
blessings of the Priesthood through their husbands. This
emphasizes very strongly the importance of marriage.
Every woman in the church, of mature age, and worthi-
ness, who is ambitious to attain to exaltation and glory
hereafter should be married, should be sealed to a man
for time and all eternity; and we trust that the young
women of the Church as well as the young men of the
Church realize the responsibility of this important ordi-
nance. (Conf. Rept., April 1921, p. 24)

The Heber J. Grant presidency continued the trend in 1922:

*Women, **not being heirs to the priesthood** except*
*as they enjoy and participate in its **blessings** through*
their husbands, are not identified with the priesthood
quorums, and consequently do not receive the religious
instruction and training imparted at quorum meetings.
*(**Mess. of First Pres**. 5:217)*

Again, in 1926, this same position was reiterated in an
interesting pamphlet printed by the Deseret News Press:

Women do not hold the priesthood, but they do
share equally in the blessings and gifts bestowed
on the priesthood in temple courts, in civic, social and
domestic life. "The man is not without the woman in the
Lord, nor the woman without the man." So said Paul,
and so taught Joseph Smith.
Office and priesthood carry heavy responsibilities
requiring constant labor and time. No woman could safe-
*ly carry the **triple burden** of wifehood, motherhood,*
and at the same time function in priestly orders. Yet her
creative home labor ranks side by side, in earthly and
heavenly importance, with her husband's priestly
responsibilities. His is the marketplace—hers at the
hearthstone. ("Women of the 'Mormon' Church." Susa
Young Gates and Leah D. Widtsoe, p. 5)

The question might well be asked at this point, how can a man, then, be expected to carry the "triple burden" of husbandhood, fatherhood, and still "function in priestly orders?" This line of reasoning seems quite shallow.

In 1952 Stephen L. Richards, first counselor in the First Presidency, reaffirmed that—

> **A woman does not hold the priesthood**, but she shares it with her husband, and she is the immediate beneficiary of many of its great blessings. When she unites in marriage with a man of the priesthood in one of the temples of the kingdom, the blessings pronounced upon her are of equal import to those given her husband, and these blessings are to be realized only through the enduring compact of the marriage. (**Conf. Rept.**, Oct. 1952, p. 99)

A 1956 conference talk by J. Reuben Clark, Jr., expresses his belief that women did not receive Priesthood:

> I have always thought that there was in this an indication of the Priesthood status of women, because of the punishment which apparently was inflicted upon Aaron, which differed from the punishment which was inflicted upon Miriam—that here was an indication that **women did not receive the Priesthood, and certainly so far as we know, women have not had the Priesthood**. Miriam's punishment may have covered her seeming claim that she had a right to Priesthood powers. (**Conf. Rept.**, Oct. 1956, p. 85)

A discussion on the history of any gospel subject would be incomplete without comments from Bruce R. McConkie:

> There is no such thing in the true Church as a high priestess. Where this office is found in a church, it is an unauthorized and apostate innovation. **Women do not hold the priesthood**. (**Mor. Doc.**, p. 355)

Women do not have the priesthood conferred upon them and are not ordained to offices therein, but they are entitled to all priesthood blessings. Those women who go on to their exaltation, ruling and reigning with husbands who are kings and priests, will themselves be queens and priestesses. They will hold positions of power, authority, and preferment in eternity. **(Mor. Doc.**, p. 594)

And in 1963 William J. Critchlow presented his views in General Conference:

Priesthood is for men only—it is not conferred upon women. The sisters may be set apart as officers in the Priesthood auxiliaries, but they are never ordained to office in the Priesthood. **They do not share the Priesthood with their husbands, fathers, or sons.** They do share the **blessings** of the Priesthood with their husbands, fathers, or sons. They do share the blessings with their husbands; sealed in a temple, they go along hand in hand with them toward exaltation, finally reigning as "queens and priestesses" with their husbands who become "kings and priests." (D & C 94:41) Infrequently a sister asks, Why can't we (sisters) hold the Priesthood? My answer: If and when he whose business Priesthood is wants you to hold it, he will let his prophet know. Until then there is nothing we can do about it. **(Conf. Rept.**, Oct. 1963, p. 29)

While these gentlemen do have a technical point that women do not have the Melchizedek Priesthood conferred upon them, these brethren seem to enjoy putting women in a subordinate role to men; whereas before the turn of the century, women had achieved a little higher station. Where once it was taught that women held the Priesthood in conjunction with their husbands, this was changed to women sharing only the **blessings** of the Priesthood in conjunction with their husbands.

When the Church changes its "eternal" doctrines, ordinances and laws (such as their stand on woman and the Priesthood), it can mean one of two things: either they were in error in the past and have repented, or their origins were correct and new changes are making them go astray.

During the same month in which the Church made the official declaration for blacks to receive the Priesthood, Spencer Kimball also stated, "We pray to God to reveal his mind and we always will, but we don't expect any revelation regarding women and the Priesthood." ("Kimball Says No Women in Priesthood", **S.L. Tribune,** June 13, 1978, D-1)

President Kimball had access to all the historical and doctrinal records of the Church which stated that black men should not receive the Priesthood; but he tried to give it to them anyway. Then with access to similar records stating that women already hold the Priesthood with their husbands, he believed it would take a special revelation for that to occur, but he doesn't expect to receive one. Here is a man who tried to give Priesthood where it shouldn't be given, and refused to acknowledge Priesthood where it already is!

A recent article about Mitt Romney (George Romney's son), who is the 1994 Mormon Republican senatorial candidate in Massachusetts, referred to the LDS Church stand of not allowing women to hold Priesthood. It was reported:

Mitt Romney would not comment on the Mormon Church's policy of barring women from the priesthood.

"Has Sen. Kennedy stood up to the pope and said: `It's just not right. We need women priests'? If he has, I will listen. I do not consider it my place as a member of my church to fly out to Salt Lake City and say: `You, who are people I believe in and trust, are wrong out here. Let me tell you how you should run your church. You should have women in the priesthood,'" Romney said. * * *

Late last year, Romney ordered the removal of a woman from the post of Sunday School president after higher church officials in Salt Lake City said the post should be held only by men.

*Romney said he only was following orders in having the woman removed. He also said he gave the title to a man but allowed the woman to retain the real responsibilities and do the work. (**S.L. Tribune**, front page, Sept. 8, 1994)*

The last two paragraphs of this article just add fuel to the LDS feminists' fire!

The question continues to be asked in Mormon and non-Mormon circles: "Will such media coverage and direct or indirect pressure from an increasing number of LDS members result in a change in the current LDS Church position regarding women and the priesthood?

* * *

Women who do not marry a Priesthood holder place themselves under certain Gospel restrictions. For example, John A. Widtsoe stated:

*Women married to non-members of the Church should not receive their temple endowments. (**Prst. & Ch. Gov.**, p. 343)*

It is obvious then, that a woman can hold or share no greater Priesthood than that which her husband possesses. If he has obtained only the Aaronic Priesthood, then she is restricted to that same power and authority.

Chapter 10

PRIESTHOOD
"PRIVILEGES, BLESSINGS AND GIFTS"

Gifts of the Priesthood

According to Joseph Smith, "the sisters would come in possession of the privileges, blessings and gifts of the Priesthood, and that signs should follow them." (DHC 4:602) Edward Tullidge beautifully describes some of these great gifts and privileges of righteous LDS sisters who share in this Priesthood authority:

> The sisters were quite as familiar with angelic visitors as the apostles. They were in fact the best "mediums" of this spiritual work. They were the "cloud of witnesses." Their Pentecosts of spiritual gifts were of frequent occurrence.
>
> The sisters were also apostolic in a priestly sense. They partook of the priesthood equally with the men. They, too, "held the keys of the administration of angels." * * *
>
> Woman also soon became high priestess and prophetess. She was this officially. The constitution of the Church acknowledged her divine mission to administer for the regeneration of the race. The genius of a patriarchal priesthood naturally made her the apostolic help-meet for man. If you saw her not in the pulpit teaching the congregation, yet was she to be found in the temple, administering for the living and the dead! Even in the holy of holies she was met. As a high

146

priestess she blessed with the laying on of hands! As a prophetess she oracled in holy places! As an endowment giver she was a Mason, of the Hebraic order, whose Grand Master is the God of Israel and whose anointer is the Holy Ghost.

*She held the keys of the administration of angels and of the working of miracles and of the "sealings" pertaining to "the heavens and the earth." Never before was woman so much as she is in this Mormon dispensation! (**Women of Mormondom**, Tullidge, pp. 22-23)*

Tullidge goes on to give an example of how some Relief Society sisters exercised the power of their Priesthood:

*It should be recorded, as unique in history, that the laying of the corner-stone of this building was performed by the ladies. This ceremony, being unostentatiously performed, was followed by appropriate speechmaking on the part of the presiding officer of the society, Mrs. S. M. Kimball, Eliza R. Snow, and others; each in turn mounting the corner-stone for a rostrum, and each winning deserved applause from the assembled thousands. (**Ibid.**, p. 491)*

As one of the most outspoken supporters of the position that women held the Priesthood in the early days of the restoration, Edward Tullidge explained:

*The Mormon women, as well as men, hold the priesthood. To all that man attains, in celestial exaltation and glory, woman attains. She is his partner in estate and office. (**Ibid.**, p. 487)*

Then regarding the second anointing, Tullidge continued:

*In the Mormon temple, woman is not merely implied, but well defined and named. There the theme of the song of the New Jerusalem is faithfully rendered in her personality. If man is anointed priest unto God, woman is anointed priestess; if symboled in his heavenly estate as king, she is also symboled as queen. (**Ibid.**, p. 488)*

In 1899 an interesting example of women giving blessings is recorded in the diaries of L. John Nuttall:

> Bro. Maeser dictated & I wrote our report to the S S
> Board, Sister Woolf & counsilors Hamman & June E
> Bates. Sisters Rhoda Hamman and several other sisters
> called & we conversed on Relief Society matters. I
> explained many things to them & they were much
> pleased after which Sister Elizabeth Hamman said she
> felt the same spirit which was upon her at the meeting
> last night when she wanted to bless me. She arose &
> placed her hands on Bro. Maeser's head & blessed him,
> then on my head & blessed me, then on Sister Woolf &
> blessed her; also blessed 3 other of the sisters & sister
> Zina Card. This was done in tongues—Sister Zina Y.
> Card arose and laying her hands on our heads interpret-
> ed these bless(ings). A good feeling was present. (Aug. 7,
> 1899)

What reaction would there be if such a thing occurred
today? What would Church leaders say if they found out
a woman gave a blessing to a man? What would the leaders say if some women spoke or sang in tongues?
Certainly there would not be "a good feeling" among
them.

Some male Priesthood holders have thought that they
are the only ones of their household entitled to receive
revelation. They sneer at the idea of women receiving it;
but Orson Pratt explained that it was common anciently
for women to enjoy this spiritual gift:

> The Lord used to give revelation not only to the head
> of a family, but also to a man's wives. Read, for
> instance, what the Lord revealed to the wives of Jacob,
> how he used to reveal a great many things to Rachel, a
> great many things to Leah, a great many things to

Bilhah, and a great many things to Zilpah. These four wives were revelators; they were prophetesses; they were individuals that could inquire of the Lord, and obtain an answer from him; and we have their revelations recorded in the Scriptures. We call their revelations the Word of God to them. What a benefit it would be for a man who had three or four or half a dozen wives, who could receive the word of the Lord in relation to their several duties; how calculated it would be to produce peace, and union, and salvation in the family and household. (JD 20:67)

When someone is baptized and confirmed a member of the Church, he or she is promised the gift of the Holy Ghost. Both men and women can and should enjoy the blessings and gifts resulting therefrom, as the Prophet Joseph Smith said:

We believe in the gift of the Holy Ghost being enjoyed now, as much as it was in the Apostles' days; ... we also believe in prophecy, in tongues, in visions, and in revelations, in gifts, and in healings; and that these things cannot be enjoyed without the gift of the Holy Ghost. * * *
We believe that the Holy Ghost is imparted by the laying on of hands of those in authority, and that the gift of tongues, and also the gift of prophecy are gifts of the Spirit, and are obtained through that medium. (TPJS, p. 243)

Heber C. Kimball also mentioned that these gifts of the Holy Ghost were certainly not restricted to just male members:

*When the Holy Ghost dwells in us, it will enable us to discern between right and wrong, will show us things to come, and bring things to our remembrance, and will make every one of this people prophets and **prophetesses** of God. (JD 4:119)*

Gift of Healing

One of the most noted and frequently exercised spiritual gifts among women in the Church has been the gift of healing. There have been a few individuals, however, that refused to grant women that privilege. In 1884 the following comments were recorded by a counselor in the Salt Lake Stake Presidency:

> *The stake counselor next expressed his own discomfort with "sisters who claim they have been blessed and set apart by the authority of God to anoint the sick of their own sex." He emphasized that each LDS woman "holds Priesthood in connection with her husband, but not separate from him." He concluded with a tirade against the "vain ambition" and "grave mistakes some of our sisters have made in seeking to raise herself [sic] to an equality with man in all things." (Joseph E. Taylor, S.L. Stake Historical Minutes, Jan. 30, 1884, LDS Archives; as quoted in Michael Quinn's article in* **Women and Authority***, p. 379)*

He must not have been familiar with Joseph Smith's instructions that it was permissible for women to perform healing blessings—as supported by the following:

> *Respecting females administering for the healing of the sick, he (Joseph Smith) further remarked, there could be no evil in it, if God gave His sanction by healing; that there could be no more sin in any female laying hands on and praying for the sick, than in wetting the face with water; it is no sin for anybody to administer that has faith, or if the sick have faith to be healed by their administration (DHC 4:604)*

And again:

> *Joseph Smith made a point of the fact that faithful women, as well as men, could enjoy the spiritual gifts*

*and powers of the gospel, and exercise spiritual gifts to bless and benefit others. In speaking to the Female Relief Society at Nauvoo, he noted that some foolish things were being circulated "against some sisters not doing right by laying hands on the sick." He countered by citing the promise of Jesus, in Mark 16:16-18, that signs and gifts were to follow those who believed, then observed: "No matter who believeth, these signs, such as **healing the sick**, casting out devils, etc., should follow all that believed, whether male or **female**. (DHC 4:603) (**Doc. of the Kingdom**, Andrus, p. 411)*

The above sentiments by the Prophet Joseph are related in more detail by Pres. Franklin D. Richards, in his July 19, 1888, discourse to the Relief Society in Ogden, Utah:

*He (Joseph Smith) said, in relation to the females administering to the sick, that there could be no more wrong in it, than in performing any other ordinance of the Church if the Lord gave His sanction by healing the sick under the hands of the sisters. * * ***

*He (J.S.) said the reason of these remarks being made was, that some little foolish things were circulating in the society, against some sisters not doing right in laying hands on the sick. Said if the people had common sympathies they would rejoice that the sick could be healed; that the time had not been before that these things could be in their proper order; that the church is not fully organized in its proper order, and cannot be until the Temple is completed, where places will be provided for the administration of the ordinances of the Priesthood. * * ***

President (Joseph) Smith then gave instruction respecting the propriety of females administering to the sick by the prayer of faith, and laying on of hands, or the anointing with oil; and said it was according to revelation that the sick should be nursed with herbs and mild food, and not by the hand of an enemy. Who are better qualified to administer than our faithful and zealous sisters whose hearts are full of faith, tenderness, *sympathy, and compassion. No one. Said he was never placed in similar circumstances before, and never had given the same instruction; and closed his instructions by expressing his heartfelt satisfaction in improving this opportunity. * * **

*I wish all the sisters were so faithful that they were healers of the sick, through the power of God. (****Coll. Dis***. 5:18-19)*

Brigham Young also encouraged the sisters to administer to the sick—especially to their own children:

It is the privilege of a mother to have faith and to administer to her child; this she can do herself as well as sending for the Elders to have the benefit of their faith. (JD 13:155)

One of the first examples in our dispensation of a woman's gift of healing was that of Sarah S. Leavitt, who healed her daughter, Louisa, of a lengthy illness:

(I) prayed earnestly to the Lord to let us know what we should do. There was an angel stood by my bed to answer my prayer. He told me to call Louisa up and lay my hands upon her head in the name of Jesus Christ and administer to her and she should recover. I awakened my husband, who lay by my side, and told him to get up, make a fire, and get Louisa up. She would hear to him sooner than to me; to tell her that an angel had told me to lay my hands upon her head in the name of the Lord Jesus Christ and administer to her in His name and she should recover. She was perfectly ignorant of Mormonism; all she had ever heard about it was in Kirtland, what few days we stayed there and what we had told her. Her mind was weak, indeed, but she got up and I administered to her in faith, having the gift from the Lord. It was about midnight when this was done, and she began to recover from that time and was soon up and about, and the honor, praise and glory be to God and the Lamb.

*(**Note:** Sarah's husband was apparently not a member of the Church at this time.) (Taken from **Auto-biographies of Mormon Pioneer Women**, Vol 1, pp. 16-17)*

Mary Ellen Able Kimball (a wife of Heber C. Kimball) also had a healing experience where on March 2, 1857, she washed and anointed a sick woman, Susannah, who immediately felt better. After returning home, she recorded in her journal:

*I thought of the instructions I had received from time to time that the priesthood was not bestowed upon woman. I accordingly asked Mr. [Heber C.] Kimball if women had a right to wash and anoint the sick for the recovery of their health or is it a mockery in them to do so. He replied inasmuch as they are obedient to their husbands, they have a right to administer in that way in the name of the Lord Jesus Christ, but not by authority of the priesthood invested in them for that authority is not given to women. **He also said they might administer by the authority given to their husbands inasmuch as they were one with their husband.** (Journal of Mary Ellen Kimball, pub. by Pioneer Press, 1994, p. 47)*

Many such healings were experienced by the early LDS sisters, and they were encouraged by the leading brethren. John Taylor said:

*When your husbands are absent, you sisters should ask GodÕs blessing that He should lead you in the paths of life; and further, you should lay hands on your sick children and rebuke diseases in faith and power, and God will be near you. . . . (**Woman's Exponent** 5:148-49)*

Apostle Ezra T. Benson told the Saints in 1852—

The priests in Christendom warn their flocks not to believe in "Mormonism"; and yet you sisters have *power to heal the sick, by the laying on of hands, which they cannot do. (**Mill. Star** 15:130)*

Thirteen years later, Elder Benson is reported to have encouraged "ordained" women in their gift of healing:

*The year before (1865) in Cache Valley, Apostle Ezra T. Benson had called on women who had been "ordained" and held "the power to rebuke diseases" to do so, and urged all the women to gain "the same power" by "exercising faith." The record does not specify who the ordained women were or who ordained them, implying that they were well known in the community. (Newell, op. cit., p. 28 of **Women and Authority**)*

Linda Newell mentions an interesting difference of opinion that developed after 1855:

*Two differing points of view were now in print. Eliza Snow and the First Presidency agreed that the Relief Society could perform healings for women and for family. However, the First Presidency implied that the ordinance should be limited to the woman's immediate family. In contrast Eliza Snow said nothing of limiting administrations to the family and that only women who had been endowed might officiate. (Newell, op. cit., pp. 30-31 of **Women and Authority**)*

Sister Eliza R. Snow addressed another question:

*"Is it necessary for sisters to be set apart to officiate in the sacred ordinances of washing, anointing, and laying on of hands in administering to the sick?" Her answer: "Any and all sisters who honor their holy endowments, not only have the right, but should feel it a duty, whenever called upon to administer to our sisters in these ordinances, which God has graciously committed to His daughters as well as to His sons." (**Woman's Exponent** 13:61, Sept. 15, 1884)*

Emmeline B. Wells, who was soon to be president of the Relief Society, asked Wilford Woodruff about washings and anointings. He answered that—

> . . . the ordinance of washing and anointing is one that should only be administered in Temples or other holy places which are dedicated to the purpose of giving endowments to the Saints. . . . washing and anointing sisters who are approaching their confinement . . . is not, strictly speaking, an ordinance, unless it be done under the direction of the priesthood and in connection with the ordinance of laying on of hands for the restoration of the sick.
>
> There is no impropriety in sisters washing and anointing their sisters in this way, . . . but it should be understood that they do this, **not as members of the priesthood, but as members of the Church, exercising faith** for, and asking the blessings of the Lord upon, their sisters, just as they, and every member of the Church, might do in behalf of the members of their families. (Correspondence of the First Presidency, LDS Archives, April 27, 1888)

> President Woodruff distinguished between temple washings and anointings, the women's practice of washing and anointing, and the priesthood ordinance of anointing in connection with healing. Still this confirmed that the same act was performed and very nearly the same words used in the temple and outside the temple by women, and by men administering to women. (Newell, op. cit., p. 31 of **Women and Authority**)

Nevertheless, women were cautioned in their use of this healing gift and power, as Angus Cannon warned in 1878:

> The sisters have a right to anoint the sick, and pray the Father to heal them, and to exercise that faith that will prevail with God; but women must be careful how they use the **authority of the priesthood** in

*administering to the sick. (**Woman's Exponent** 13:61, Sept. 15, 1884)*

But just because a woman may have this gift and power of healing, it gives her no right to criticize her husband. Heber C. Kimball warned:

> *Some of you, ladies, that go abroad from house to house, **blessing the sick**, having your little circles of women come together, why are you troubling yourselves to bless and lay your hands on women, and prophesy on them, if you do not believe the principle? You make yourselves fools to say that that same power should not be on the man that has got the Priesthood, and with sisters that have not got any, only what they hold in connection with their husbands.*
>
> *We can tell what will come to pass; and one of you can talk in tongues and pour out your souls to God, and then one interpret; that is the course you take, and it is all right; go ahead, and God bless you and multiply blessings on you; but do not go round tattling about your husbands and talking against the Priesthood you are connected to. I do not say many of you do it; but you that do it are poor, miserable skunks. (JD 5:176-77)*

Linda Newell relates how Church acceptance of women's healing authority started to decline after the turn of the century:

> *Despite growing ambiguity as the nineteenth century closed, the leading sisters had successfully maintained their right to exercise the gift of blessing and had been supported by the church hierarchy. The twentieth century would see a definite shift.*
>
> *Louisa "Lula" Greene Richards, former editor of Women's Exponent, wrote a somewhat terse letter to President Lorenzo Snow on 9 April 1901 concerning an article she had read in the Deseret News. It had stated: "Priest, Teacher or Deacon may administer to*

the sick, and so may a member, male or female, but neither of them can seal the anointing and blessing,
because the authority to do that is vested in the
Priesthood after the order of Melchizedek." *Lula wrote:*

*"If the information given in the answer is absolutely
correct, then myself and thousands of other members of
the Church have been misinstructed and are laboring
under a very serious mistake, which certainly should be
authoritatively corrected. Sister Eliza R. Snow Smith,
from the Prophet Joseph Smith, her husband, taught the
sisters in her day, that a very important part of the
sacred ordinance of administering to the sick was the
sealing of the anointing and blessings, and should never
be omitted. and we follow the pattern she gave us continually.* **We do not seal in the authority of the
Priesthood, but in the name of our Lord and
Savior, Jesus Christ."** *(Letter in LDS Archives) (Newell,
op. cit., pp. 31-32 of Women and Authority)*

The trend continued, and Apostle Joseph Fielding
Smith stated:

The Brethren ***do not consider it necessary or wise
for the women of the Relief Society to wash and
anoint women who are sick.*** *The Lord has given us
directions in matters of this kind; we are to call in the
Elders, and they are to anoint with oil on the head and
bless by the laying on of hands.*

*The Church teaches that a woman may lay on hands
upon the head of a sick child and ask the Lord to bless
it, in the case when those holding the Priesthood cannot
be present. A man might under such conditions invite his
wife to lay on hands with him in blessing their sick child.
This would be merely to exercise her faith and not
because of any inherent right to lay on hands. A woman
would have no authority to anoint or seal a blessing,
and where Elders can be called in, that would be the
proper way to have an administration performed. (**Doc.
of Sal.** 3:178)*

In 1936 Joseph Fielding Smith wrote to Relief Society President, Belle Spafford and her counselors:

> *While the authorities of the Church have ruled that it is permissible, under certain conditions and with the* **approval of the priesthood**, *for sisters to wash and anoint other sisters, yet they feel that it is far better for us to follow* **the plan the Lord has given us** *and send for the Elders of the Church to come and administer to the sick and afflicted. (**Mess. of 1st Pres**. 4:314)*
>
> *It would certainly be difficult for a sister to say that she did not wish to follow "the plan the Lord has given us" by asking for administrations from sisters rather than elders.*
>
> *Joseph Fielding Smith officially ended women's blessings where they had not already stopped. (Newell, op. cit., pp. 40-41 of Women and Authority)*

Linda Newell's entire article, "The Historical Relationship of Mormon Women and Priesthood," pages 23-48 of **Women and Authority**, compiled by Maxine Hanks, is very worthwhile reading.

According to Orson Pratt, the true Church of Jesus Christ should have the same organization and the same gifts as it did in ancient times:

> *When I speak of the everlasting Gospel, I mean the same one that was preached eighteen hundred years ago; and authority will be given to some of the children of men to preach that everlasting Gospel among the nations; and when that shall take place, I have no doubt but what there will be many Prophets raised up, because the true Christian Church has always been characterized by Prophets.* **There never was a genuine Christian Church unless it had Prophets and Prophetesses**; *indeed, in ancient times Prophets were so numerous in one branch of the Christian Church, that Paul had to set them in order,*

and send them an epistle and tell them not to all get up and prophecy at once, but that if a thing was revealed to any one, he was not to get up and declare it while another one was speaking, but he was to wait until the first got through speaking, and then he should prophesy; for, said Paul, the spirit of the Prophets is subject to the Prophets. That is, when the spirit came upon Prophets in ancient times, it did not exercise a supernatural power upon them to force them from their seats to stand up and declare their prophecies the moment they were revealed, but that the spirit that was given to them was subject to them, so that they could stay upon their seats until the first Prophets got through prophesying. That was the order of the Christian Church when God ever had one upon the earth—Prophets were very numerous in that church.

*But by and by the time came when the Christian Church apostatized and turned away, and began to follow after their own wisdom, and the Prophets and Apostles ceased, so far as the affairs of the Christian Church on the earth were concerned. **Revelations, and visions, and the various gifts of the spirit were also taken away, according to their unbelief and apostasy.***

*. . . and if you ever see a Church arise, calling itself a Christian Church, and it has not inspired Apostles like those in ancient times, you may know that it is a spurious church, and that it makes pretensions to something that it does not enjoy. If you ever find a church called a Christian Church that has no men to foretell future events, you may know, at once, that it is not a Christian Church. If you find a Christian Church that has not the ancient gifts, for instance the **gift of healing**, opening the eyes of the blind, unstopping the ears of the deaf, causing the tongue of the dumb to speak and the lame to walk; if you ever find a people calling themselves a Christian Church and **they have not these gifts among them, you may know with a perfect knowledge that they do not agree with the pattern given in the New Testament**. (JD 18:171)*

It stands to reason that if the early Christian church had prophets and prophetesses, and gifts of the spirit exercised by both men and women, that as members of the true Church of Jesus Christ, we should be experiencing such blessings today. According to Orson Pratt, if such gifts are not in existence, then it is not the same, true church.

Chapter 11

THEIR FINEST HOUR

It is inspiring and informative to read the stories of early LDS women who, from their heart and mind, delivered some of the most noble speeches for freedom ever recorded. Here in Salt Lake City, on a very inclement 13th of January in 1870, about five or six thousand women packed the old tabernacle to present their feelings and support for what they considered to be a vitally important Priesthood law—plural marriage.

The Mormons had been suffering from the efforts of vicious mobs, prejudiced ministers, and corrupt politicians. Laws were being passed against the rights of the Mormons to live their religion unmolested. The sisters of the Church wanted to make their stand. Only women were allowed to attend these statewide mass meetings— except for a few press reporters.

Mrs. Sarah M. Kimball, as president, was the first speaker. Excerpts from her talk, as well as the remarks of several others, are reprinted here as they appeared in Tullidge's **Women of Mormondom**, showing the valiant defense of these pioneer women in behalf of this eternal Priesthood law:

> *We are not here to advocate woman's rights, but man's rights. The bill in question would not only deprive our fathers, husbands and brothers, of enjoying the privileges bequeathed to citizens of the United States,*

but it would deprive us, as women, of the privilege of selecting our husbands; and against this we unqualifiedly protest. (Sarah M. Kimball, p. 381)

Bathsheba W. Smith remarked:

I watched by the bedside of the first apostle, David W. Patten, who fell a martyr in the Church. He was a noble soul. He was shot by a mob while defending the saints in the State of Missouri. * * *

I was intimately acquainted with the life and ministry of our beloved prophet, Joseph, and our patriarch, Hyrum Smith. I know that they were pure men who labored for the redemption of the human family. For six years I heard their public and private teachings. It was from their lips that I heard taught the principle of celestial marriage; and when I saw their mangled forms cold in death, having been slain for the testimony of Jesus, by the hands of cruel bigots, in defiance of law, justice and executive pledges; . . . I realized that they had sealed their ministry with their blood, and that their testimony was in force.

On the 9th day of February, 1846—the middle of a cold and bleak winter—my husband, just rising from a bed of sickness, and I, in company with thousands of saints, were driven again from our comfortable home— the accumulation of six years' industry and prudence— and, with the little children, commenced a long and weary journey through the wilderness, to seek another home; for a wicked mob had decreed we must leave. Governor Ford, of Illinois, said the laws were powerless to protect us. Exposed to the cold of winter and the storms of spring, we continued our journey, amid want and exposure, burying by the wayside a dead mother, a son, and many kind friends and relatives.

We reached the Missouri River in July. Here our country thought proper to make a requisition upon us for a battalion to defend our national flag in the war pending with Mexico. We responded promptly, many of our kindred stepping forward and performing a journey

characterized by their commanding officer as unparal-
leled in history. With most of our youths and middle-
aged men gone, we could not proceed; hence we were
compelled to make another home, which, though hum-
ble, approaching winter made very desirable. In 1847-8,
all who were able, through selling their surplus proper-
ty, proceeded; we who remained were told, by an unfeel-
ing Indian department, we must vacate our houses and
recross the Missouri River, as the laws would not permit
us to remain on Indian lands! We obeyed, and again
made a new home, though only a few miles distant. The
latter home we abandoned in 1849, for the purpose of
joining our co-religionists in the then far-off region,
denominated on the map "the Great American Desert", .
. . and had found an asylum in such an undesirable
country, as to strengthen us in the hope that . . . no one
could feel heartless enough to withhold from us that reli-
gious liberty which we had sought in vain amongst our
former neighbors. * * *

I cannot but express my surprise, mingled with regret
and indignation, at the recent efforts of ignorant, bigot-
ed, and unfeeling men—headed by the Vice-President—
to aid intolerant sectarians and reckless speculators,
who seek for proscription and plunder, and who feel
willing to rob the inhabitants of these valleys of their
hard-earned possessions, and, what is dearer, the con-
stitutional boon of religious liberty. (Bathsheba W.
Smith, pp. 381-384)

Sister Warren Smith, a survivor of the Haun's Mill massacre, reiterated that tragic story and then said:

We are here today to say, if such scenes shall be
again enacted in our midst, I say to you, my sisters, you
are American citizens; let us stand by the truth, if we die
for it. (Sister Warren Smith, p. 386)

Mrs. Wilmarth East then spoke:

It is with feelings of pleasure, mingled with indigna-
tion and disgust, that I appear before my sisters, to

express my feelings in regard to the Cullom Bill, now before the Congress of this once happy republican government. The constitution for which our forefathers fought and bled and died, bequeaths to us the right of religious liberty—the right to worship God according to the dictates of our own conscience! Does the Cullom Bill give us this right? Compare it with the constitution, if you please, and see what a disgrace has come upon this once happy and republican government!

Where, O, where, is that liberty, bequeathed to us by our forefathers—the richest boon ever given to man or woman, except eternal life, or the gospel of the Son of God? I am an American citizen by birth. Having lived under the laws of the land, I claim the right to worship God according to the dictates of my conscience, and the commandments that God shall give unto me.

Our constitution guarantees life, liberty, and the pursuit of happiness, to all who live beneath it. What is life to me, if I see the galling yoke of oppression placed on the necks of my husband, sons and brothers, as Mr. Cullom would have it? I am proud to say to you that I am not only a citizen of the United States of America, but a citizen of the kingdom of God, and the laws of this kingdom I am willing to sustain and defend both by example and precept. (Mrs. Wilmarth East, pp. 386-87)

Sister Eliza R. Snow also addressed the meeting:

The entrance of our brave pioneers, and the settlement of the Latter-day Saints in these mountain vales, which then were only barren, savage wilds, are events with which not only our own future, but the future of the whole world, is deeply associated.

Here they struggled, with more than mortal energy, for their hearts and hands were nerved by the spirit of the Most High, and through His blessings they succeeded in drawing sustenance from the arid soils; here they erected the standard on which the star-spangled banner waved its salutation of welcome to the nations of the earth; and here it will be bequeathed, unsullied, to future generations. Yes, that "dear old flag" which in my girlhood I always contemplated with joyous pride, and to which the patriotic strains of my earliest muse were chanted, here floats triumphantly on the mountain breeze.

Our numbers, small at first, have increased, until now we number one hundred and fifty thousand; and yet we are allowed only a territorial government. Year after year we have petitioned Congress for that which is our inalienable right to claim—a State government; and, year after year, our petitions have been treated with contempt. Such treatment as we have received from our rulers, has no precedent in the annals of history.

And now, instead of granting us our rights as American citizens, bills are being presented to Congress, which are a disgrace to men in responsible stations, professing the least claim to honor and magnanimity; bills which, if carried into effect, would utterly annihilate us as a people. * * *

In the kingdom of God, woman has no interests separate from those of man—all are mutual.

Our enemies pretend that, in Utah, woman is held in a state of vassalage—that she does not act from choice, but by coercion—that we would even prefer life elsewhere, were it possible for us to make our escape. What nonsense! We all know that if we wished we could leave at any time—either to go singly, or to rise en masse, and there is no power here that could, or would wish to, prevent us.

I will now ask this assemblage of intelligent ladies, do you know of any place on the face of the earth, where woman has more liberty, and where she enjoys such high and glorious privileges as she does here, as a Latter-day Saint? No! The very idea of woman here in a state of slavery is a burlesque on good common sense. * * *

They must be very dull in estimating the energy of female character, who can persuade themselves that women who for the sake of their religion left their homes, crossed the plains with handcarts, or as many *had previously done, drove ox, mule and horse-teams from Nauvoo and from other points, when their husbands and sons went, at their country's call, to fight her battles in Mexico; yes, that very country which had refused us protection, and from which we were then struggling to make our escape—I say those who think that such women and the daughters of such women do not possess too much energy of character to remain passive and mute under existing circumstances, are "reckoning without their host." To suppose that we should not be aroused when our brethren are threatened with fines and imprisonment, for their faith in, and obedience to, the laws of God, is an insult to our womanly natures.*

Were we the stupid, degraded, heartbroken beings that we have been represented, silence might better become us; but as women of God, women filling high and responsible positions, performing sacred duties—women who stand not as dictators, but as counselors to their husbands, and who, in the purest, noblest sense of refined womanhood, are truly their helpmates—we not only speak because we have the right, but justice and humanity demand that we should.

My sisters, let us, inasmuch as we are free to do all that love and duty prompt, be brave and unfaltering in sustaining our brethren. Women's faith can accomplish wonders. Let us, like the devout and steadfast Miriam, assist our brothers in upholding the hands of Moses. * * *

But to the law and to the testimony. Those obnoxious fratricidal bills—I feel indignant at the thought that such documents should disgrace our national legislature. * * * They not only threaten extirpation to us, but they augur destruction to the government. The authors of those bills would tear the constitution to shreds; they are sapping the foundation of American freedom—they would obliterate every vestige of the dearest right of man—liberty of conscience—and reduce our once happy country to a state of anarchy. (Eliza R. Snow, pp. 388-393)

Next came a very powerful speech by Harriet Cook Young:

*In rising to address this meeting, delicacy prompts me to explain the chief motives which have dictated our present action. We, the ladies of Salt Lake City, have assembled here today, not for the purpose of assuming any particular political power, nor to claim any special prerogative which may or may not belong to our sex; but to express our indignation at the unhallowed efforts of men, who, regardless of every principle of manhood, justice, and constitutional liberty, would force upon a religious community, by a direct issue, either the course of apostasy, or the bitter alternative of fire and sword. Surely the instinct of self-preservation, the love of liberty and happiness, and the right to worship God, are dear to our sex as well as to the other; and when these most sacred of all rights are thus wickedly assailed, it becomes absolutely our duty to defend them. * * **

Let the world know that the women of Utah prefer virtue to vice, and the home of an honorable wife to the gilded pageantry of fashionable temples of sin. Transitory allurements, glaring the senses, as is the flame to the moth, short-lived and cruel in their results, possess no charms for us. Every woman in Utah may have her husband—the husband of her choice. Here we are taught not to destroy our children, but to preserve them, for they, reared in the path of virtue and trained to righteousness, constitute our true glory.

It is with no wish to accuse our sisters who are not of our faith that we so speak; but we are dealing with facts as they exist. Wherever monogamy reigns, adultery, prostitution and foeticide, directly or in-directly, are its concomitants. It is not enough to say that the virtuous and highminded frown upon these evils. We believe they do. But frowning upon them does not cure them; it does not even check their rapid growth; either the remedy is too weak, or the disease is too strong. The women of Utah comprehend this; and they see, in the principle of plurality of wives, the *only safeguard against adultery, prostitution, and the reckless waste of pre-natal life, practiced throughout the land. * * ***

While these are our views, every attempt to force that obnoxious measure upon us must of necessity be an attempt to coerce us in our religious and moral convictions, against which did we not most solemnly protest, we would be unworthy the name of American women. (Harriet Cook Young, pp. 394, 396-97)

Sister Hannah T. King followed with a stinging address directed to General Cullom himself:

My sisters, are we really in America—the world-renowned land of liberty, freedom, and equal rights?—the land of which I dreamed, in my youth, as being almost an earthly elysium, where freedom of thought and religious liberty were open to all!—the land that Columbus wore his noble life out to discover!!—the land that God himself helped him to exhume, and to aid, which endeavor Isabella, a queen, a woman, declared she would pawn her jewels and crown of Castile, to give him the outfit that he needed!—the land of Washington, the Father of his Country, and a host of noble spirits, too numerous to mention!—the land to which the Mayflower bore the pilgrim fathers, who rose up and left their homes, and bade their native home "good night", simply that they might worship God by a purer and holier faith, in a land of freedom and liberty, of which the name America has long been synonymous! Yes, my sisters, this is America, but, oh, how are the mighty fallen!

Who, or what, is the creature who framed this incomparable document! Is he an Esquimaux or a chimpanzee? What isolated land or spot produced him? What ideas he must have of women! Had he ever a mother, a wife, or a sister? In what academy was he tutored, or to what school does he belong, that he so coolly and systematically commands the women of this people to turn traitors to their husbands, their brothers, and their sons? Short-sighted man "sections" and "the bill!" Let us, the women of this people—the sisterhood of Utah—rise en masse, and tell this nondescript to defer "the bill" until he has studied the character of woman, such as God intended she should be; then he will discover that devotion, veneration and faithfulness are her peculiar attributes; that God is her refuge, and his servants her oracles; and that, especially, the women of Utah have paid too high a price for their present position, their present light and knowledge, and their noble future, to succumb to so mean and foul a thing as Baskin, Cullom & Co.'s bill. Let him learn that they are one in heart, hand and brain, with the brotherhood of Utah—that God is their father and their friend—that into His hands they commit their cause—and on their pure and simple banner they have emblazoned their motto, "God, and my right!" (Hannah T. King, pp. 397-99)

The next speaker was Phoebe Woodruff:

I have been a member of this church for thirty-six years, and had the privilege of living in the days of the Prophet Joseph, and heard his teaching for many years. He ever counseled us to honor, obey and maintain the principles of our noble constitution, for which our fathers fought, and which many of them sacrificed their lives to establish. President Brigham Young has always taught the same principle. This glorious legacy of our fathers, the Constitution of the United States, guarantees unto all the citizens of this great republic the right to worship God according to the dictates of their own consciences, as it expressly says, "Congress shall make no laws respecting an establishment of religion, or prohibiting the free exercise thereof." Cullom's bill is in direct violation of this declaration of the constitution, and I think it is our duty to do all in our power, by our voices and influence, to thwart the passage of this bill, which commits a violent outrage upon our rights, and the rights of our fathers, husbands and sons; * * *

Shall we, as wives and mothers, sit still and see our husbands and sons, whom we know are obeying the *highest behest of heaven, suffer for their religion, without exerting ourselves to the extent of our power for their deliverance? No; verily no! God has revealed unto us the law of the patriarchal order of marriage, and commanded us to obey it. We are sealed to our husbands for time and eternity, that we may dwell with them and our children in the world to come; which guarantees unto us the greatest blessing for which we are created. If the rulers of the nation will so far depart from the spirit and letter of our glorious constitution as to deprive our prophets, apostles and elders of citizenship, and imprison them for obeying this law, let them grant this, our last request, to make their prisons large enough to hold their wives, for where they go we will go also. (Phoebe Woodruff, pp. 399-400)*

Sister Eliza R. Snow gave the concluding remarks:

I heard the Prophet Joseph Smith say if the people rose and mobbed us and the authorities countenanced it, they would have mobs to their hearts' content. I heard him say that the time would come when this nation would so far depart from its original purity, its glory, and its love of freedom and protection of civil and religious rights, that the constitution of our country would hang as it were by a thread. He said, also, that this people, the sons of Zion, would rise up and save the constitution, and bear it off triumphantly. * * *

I consider it most important, my sisters, that we should struggle to preserve the sacred constitution of our country—one of the blessings of the Almighty, for the same spirit that inspired Joseph Smith, inspired the framers of the constitution; and we should ever hold it sacred, and bear it off triumphantly. (Eliza R. Snow, pp. 401-402)

What noble lives of faith and integrity these pioneer women left for men! By precept and example they displayed the finest qualities of mortal souls. They passed on the torch of liberty for later generations to carry and respect. It is up to us to continue in that path and march on in support of those eternal Priesthood goals and principles!

Chapter 12

CONCLUSION: PRIESTHOOD
POWER THROUGH OBEDIENCE

A Priesthood Problem

Where does the Priesthood issue stand today? Some women are pushing to have Priesthood conferral—something that has never been instituted for women. Some are requesting Priesthood offices such as High Priests, Bishops, Stake Presidents, etc. This, too, is not according to the revelations of God. Others want to have all things equal with men—activities in church, in government, at work, and in marriage. There are also those who seek to pray to and worship our Mother as well as (or instead of) our Father in Heaven.

Where will the misunderstandings and differences end? How can we truly understand the Priesthood plan which the Lord gave in the beginning? There are some serious problems to solve before the house of God can be set back in order.

If each Mormon partner in a marriage respects the other for what they are and the rightful position they hold in the Priesthood order, they should not have the problems that are plaguing our society today. The present generation seeks to put women and men on the same level in the marriage covenant, but this can have confusing results, as Dr. Rodney Turner describes:

*Both are president of the company. Being a two-head-ed affair, the modern marriage is, in actuality, headless. Because both preside, neither leads. It is pure democracy. Such marriages are based upon false sociological theories as well as a fatal misunderstanding of the implications of the psycho-physical differences between the sexes. These differences should dictate the valid roles of husbands and wives. In largely ignoring these differences, the modern marriage is essentially a contractual agreement between consenting adults in which they specify the limitation of their obligations to one another both qualitatively and quantitatively. It is understood that each is free to pursue his or her own destiny even though they share certain phases of their lives with one another. (**Woman and the Priesthood**, Turner, p. 69)*

Prof. Turner gave some good advice when he said:

*The spirit of envy and competition is alien to the Spirit of Christ. It is especially inappropriate where the priesthood is concerned. **It is, perhaps, a greater sin for a woman to covet a man's priesthood than it would be for her to covet anything else.** And there is no need for her to do so. Eternal marriage unites their "priesthoods" in one, making them a shared blessing. (Ibid., p. 287)*

An equal partnership is formed when each party has a 50% vote in the organization—one being able to nullify the other. When this idea is adopted in a marriage, it is no longer a loving, natural companionship, but a corporate stockholder business, and life for both usually becomes confusing, difficult, and often disastrous.

The editor of the **Millennial Star** gave some excellent advice to both wives and husbands:

Every dear wife will look with a zealous eye towards the happiness and welfare of her dear husband, and if she is tempted to think he is doing wrong, she will say, Get thee behind me, Satan; that is none of my business; I will do right, that is enough for me, and I shall have peace in my soul. And so continue to do, till he has done so wrong that forbearance is no longer a virtue, then give him a divorce and do better if you can; but while you live with him, live in peace, and keep jealousy out of doors; if you donÕt you will always have hell within, and devils enough to carry it on. The moment you are jealous that your husband is wrong, that moment you are miserable; that misery is proof positive that you yourself are wrong, for it destroys your peace. ***

Some husbands are so mighty big because they are the head, that the wife has no room in the house; if she thinks, she thinks wrong; if she speaks, she speaks wrong; if she acts, she acts wrong; she can't do a right thing for the life of her; and do what she will, no matter, she is as likely to get a cuffed ear as anything else, and a little more so; and if she should ask forgiveness, she would meet with the consoling retort from her dear lord, "yes, and you'll do the same thing again next minute." Why all this? Because the dear husband, the great lord of the house, has got so many devils in him, they make him so big there is not room for anybody else in that house. (**Mill. Star** *14:280*)

But, according to the Lord, a man cannot obtain the fullness of the powers of the Priesthood without a woman:

In the celestial glory there are three heavens or degrees; and in order to obtain the highest, a man must enter into this order of the priesthood [meaning the new and everlasting covenant of marriage]; And if he does not, he cannot obtain it. He may enter into the other, but that is the end of his kingdom; he cannot have an increase. (D & C 131:1-4)

So it appears that in this regard God is favoring women over men, as there will apparently be greater numbers of women exalted than men.

A Woman's Curse

A difficult trial in a woman's life is to live under the curse placed upon her since the days of the garden of Eden:

> *Unto the woman he said, I will greatly multiply thy sorrow and thy conception;* **in sorrow thou shalt bring forth children; and thy desire shall be to thy husband, and he shall rule over thee.** *(Gen. 3:16)*

Regarding the first part of the "curse" that "in sorrow thou shalt bring forth children," there is a resulting promise that "Notwithstanding she shall be saved in childbearing, if they continue in faith and charity and holiness with sobriety." (I Tim. 2:15) And Rodney Turner expands upon this by saying, "If a woman is saved in child-bearing, she is exalted in child-guidance." **(Wom. & Prsthd.**, p. 292)

Paul also reiterated the second part of the "curse" in his epistle to the Ephesians:

> **Wives, submit yourselves unto your own husbands,** *as unto the Lord. For the husband is the head of the wife, even as Christ is the head of the church: and he is the saviour of the body. Therefore as the church is subject unto Christ, so let the wives be to their own husbands in every thing. (Eph. 5:22-24)*

All women must live under this "curse" during her sojourn in mortality; and by realizing the fact that it is still in effect, helps to explain the apparent inequalities and injustices toward women today. Brigham Young explained this on many occasions, four of which are included here:

> *True there is a* **curse** *upon the woman that is not upon the man, namely that "her whole affections shall be towards her husband," and what is the next?* **"He shall rule over you."**

But how is it now? Your desire is to your husband, but you strive to rule over him, whereas the man should rule over you.

Some may ask whether that is the case with me; go to my house and live, and then you will learn that I am very kind, but know how to rule. (JD 4:57)

*

It may be all well enough if a woman can attain faith to throw off the curse, but there is one thing she cannot away with, at least not so far as I am concerned, and that is, "and he shall rule over thee." I can do that by causing my women to do as they have a mind to, and at the same time they do not know what is going on. When I say rule, I do not mean with an iron hand, but merely to take the lead—to lead them in the path I wish them to walk in. They may be determined not to answer my will, but they are doing it all the time without knowing it. (JD 9:195)

*

The female portion of the human family have blessings promised to them if they are faithful. I do not know what the Lord could have put upon women worse than he did upon Mother Eve, where he told her: "Thy desire shall be to thy husband," continually wanting the husband. "If you go to work, my eyes follow you; if you go away in the carriage, my eyes follow you, and I like you and love you; I delight in you, and I desire you should have nobody else." I do not know that the Lord could have put upon women anything worse than this. I do not blame them for having these feelings. I would be glad if it were otherwise. Says a woman of faith and knowledge, "I will make the best of it; it is a law that man shall rule over me; his word is my law, and I must obey him; he must rule over me; this is upon me and I will submit to it," and by so doing she has promises that others do not have. (JD 16:167)

*

They [Adam and Eve] were required to multiply and replenish the earth, and I will here say a word to the ladies—Do not marvel, do not wonder at it, do not complain at Providence, do not find fault with mother Eve because your desire is to your husbands. Bear this with patience and fortitude! Be reconciled to it, meet your afflictions and these little—well, we might say, not very trifling, but still they are wants, for if we desire only that that is necessary, and can govern and control ourselves to be satisfied with that, it is a great deal better than to want a thousand things that are unnecessary, and especially to the female portion of the inhabitants of the earth. But there is a curse upon them, and I cannot take it off, can you? No, you cannot—it never will be taken from the human family until the mission is fulfilled, and our Master and our Lord is perfectly satisfied with our work. It will then be taken from this portion of the community, and will afflict them no more; but for the present it will afflict them. (JD 15:13)

Edward Tullidge also speaks of the time when women will be redeemed from this curse:

The day is approaching when woman shall be redeemed from the curse of Eve; and I have often thought that our daughters who are in polygamy will be the first redeemed.

Here is the curse: **"In sorrow thou shalt bring forth children; and thy desire shall be to thy husband, and he shall rule over thee!"** *Woman will be* **redeemed from that curse***, as sure as the coming of tomorrowÔs sun. No more, after this generation, shall civilized man rule over his mate, but "they twain shall be one;" and the sisters are looking for that* **millennial day***. These are the "wise virgins" of the church; and their lamps are trimmed.* **(Women of Mormondom,** *Tullidge, p. 506)*

But until that time arrives when the curse is no longer in effect, Brigham Young advises the husbands to treat their

wives "as an angel would treat them" (JD 4:55), and
counsels the wives that "a man is not made to be worshipped." (JD 14:106).

Other words of comfort come from Rodney Turner, who
softened some of the harsh interpretations of the "fall" of
Adam and Eve and presented another way of looking at
it:

> When he [Adam] accepted the forbidden fruit from his
> wifeÕs hand and joined her in mortality, she incurred a
> debt of gratitude toward the Priesthood which she
> acknowledged by humble acceptance of God's judgment
> upon her. And in honoring her husband as her temporal
> lord, in placing her womanly affections upon him alone,
> and in becoming the mother of all living, she laid down
> her life for others as Adam had laid down his life for her.
>
> Those women who do the works of Eve become, in
> fact, her eternal daughters. In emulating their ancient
> mother, they help to lift whatever curses and limitations
> the Fall has inflicted upon them. (Epilogue, **Woman and
> the Priesthood**, Turner)

Daniel H. Wells says, nevertheless, that happiness can
be obtained through a wife's righteous obedience to her
husband:

> I say to the sisters, seek to have confidence in your hus-
> bands, and believe that they are capable of leading you;
> and when you seek instruction, believe them capable of
> giving it to you; and be faithful, humble, and obedient to
> them. Their feelings should not be concentrated in you,
> but your feelings should be in them, and theirs should be
> in those who lead them in the Priesthood. Their feelings
> are concentrated in the Lord their God and what is ahead,
> and there is where they should be. You should be glad to
> see them step forward and walk onward in the path of
> their duty, and not require them to devote themselves to
> you to the exclusion of things and duties of life which lie
> before them. As they progress and lead on, you will feel to

travel in the same road. This is the order, and if order is maintained in this thing, you will see the beauty of it; and it will be a satisfaction to you and them to believe that your husband, he who is at your head, is progressing in the things of God. That should be a satisfaction to you, and it will be, if you are inspired by the right spirit and feeling. In this way you will have happiness, and see good times. (JD 4:256)

Even though the curse will be removed from women, there is still a patriarchal order that continues from this life to the next:

*The **order of heaven** places man in the front rank; hence he is first to be addressed. Woman follows under the protection of his counsels, and the superior strength of his arm. Her desire should be unto her husband, and he should rule over her. I will here venture the assertion, that no man can be exalted to a celestial glory in the kingdom of God whose wife rules over him; and as the man is not without the woman, nor the woman without the man in the Lord, it follows as a matter of course, **that the woman who rules over her husband, thereby deprives herself of a celestial glory.** (Orson Hyde, JD 4:258)*

An Encouraging Word

In conclusion, printed here are two beautiful sentiments expressed for the encouragement of women—from the pen of Eliza R. Snow. Inspiration, if not revelation, was the source of such tributes to the honor and glory of women. The first is part of an article entitled "Address to the Sisters":

It is because I love my sisters, and desire to see them maintain the position that God intended them to attain and fulfil that I now address them. It is woman's honourable privilege to be Queen of a mighty realm! Mighty in minutioe! Her "kingdom cometh not with observation," her subjects are the Lilliputians of the earth, and their moral statue will be pigmy, full *grown, or colossal, according as her laws are wise, judicious, and in love; she controls, or ought to do, the elements of life! the germs of future glory and exaltation—the rudiments of angelic life! It is her province to mould, to train, to nurture, to support, to feed, to enlighten, to sow seed into the precious mind of infancy and youth. What more noble destiny would she desire! Is she not working for eternity? most assuredly—and her work is for exaltation or condemnation—can she do this in her own strength? certainly not; let her remember, if she goes to the fountainhead of wisdom, and asks, she shall receive—to all that ask in sincerity, God giveth wisdom "liberally and upbraideth not." Many of the great men of the earth who have risen to eminence and power, have pointed to their mothers, who by their judicious management of their youth—the training of their infant minds, and the precious seed, which under God, they were enabled to cast into their minds, they became great. * * **

Shall not such instances urge woman to feel her responsibility, to consider the end of her creation? Oh! most noble is her work—mighty is her responsibility. Her first act of government must be self!—she has many a battle to fight to conquer that troublesome little empire, her own heart!—but this must be accomplished—the foundation must be good or it cannot support the superstructure. The fountain must be pure, or its streams can never fertilize the young plants that they are destined to renovate, and invigorate. The first thing she must learn and then teach is humility, the next obedience, if she wishes to conquer well, she must stoop to do so. * * *

Her soul is large enough for all her Maker intended her for, and she was made to be "a help meet for man;" these words are penned with the sublime brevity of Scripture, but they form a compendium of woman's position, of woman's duty, and of woman's exaltation; brief as they are, they stand as a text to a discourse that would fill every sheet of this "Star," but that is not for me. If woman really carries out her destiny, she is truly a heroine; if she desire greatness she has it. I will prove it, woman's sphere is in the secluded, domestic dreams of life, beyond which her name is unheard and unknown! but is he only a hero whose name resounds through the world as the herald of battle and bloodshed? in the eye of the mis-judging world such may be such, but when "the partition wall is broken down," that shuts out the mortal from the immortal, when the scales fall from the human eye, and the veil is removed from human hearts, then shall many an obscure individual stand forth as the sterling soldier of Christ, and many shall be abashed, whose proud banner flaunted over the battlefield of human glory, but who forgot to enlist themselves under the banner of the Great Captain of their salvation, and disdain to fight in the ranks of the Christian warfare. Is there no heroism in the daily, hourly, struggle of the battle of life, viz., to do our duty in the situation of life in which we are placed; in the untiring efforts to bear upward towards the light of Truth! and to keep straight in the "narrow way," that leadeth unto life, to press on "through evil report and good report," to do our duty to the wayward as well as to the kind and gentle! to be patient, to persevere, to endure, to be gentle, to be disinterested, to press on in the path of rectitude, not for the praise of men, for often no eye but God's beholds this inward struggle, and this secret strife of flesh and Spirit; but because the soul's eye is resting on that glorious promise, "be thou faithful unto death, and I will give thee a crown of life!" What is heroism if this or something of this is not a definition of it? Then I will assume that I have established the fact, that every true woman, one who has learned to govern herself and so become fit to govern others, and is swaying her sceptre according to the law of her Sovereign, is a heroine! for they must be ignorant indeed who do not know that this is but a faint outline of her struggle through life! her name will be emblazoned on no earthly scroll of fame; her brows may be bound by no coronet of bay or laurel, or diadem of gorgeous gems; but I know it is traced by the "Recording Angel" in the chancery of heaven, and sealed with the signet of the Eternal!

*Oh! my Sisters, let us again revert to the words—woman was made a "help meet for man"! Let us ponder these words in our hearts; man is the delegate of God; woman for his honour and glory! then the more glorious she is, the more honour she can confer upon him. God is the Father of all. My Sisters! let us pray then that He will given us wisdom, that we may ever act as becomes the wives, mothers, and sisters of the servants of God; that we may truly be a crown and an honour to them, and that we may stand side by side with them, as the sons and daughters of the Most High, and conjointly roll on the great work of these the last days; that having been fellow-labourers in the vineyard of the Lord, we may together inherit the glories of His kingdom, when the knowledge of the Lord shall cover the earth as the waters cover the sea, and when the Lord of Hosts shall reign in Mount Zion, and in Jerusalem, and before His ancients—gloriously. (**Mill. Star** 13:359-60)*

Eliza again counseled her sisters in the Gospel:

To be sure we have many of the crosses of life, but what do we meet them for? Are they for our own good and benefit or do we meet them all as for Zion's sake? Do we let Zion take full possession of our desire, our ambition? . . .

We have self all absorbed in the interest of the work of God. We are here to perform duties, and to do our part towards establishing God's Kingdom. We, my sisters, have as much to do as our brethren have. We are to work in union with them. . . .

Paul the Apostle anciently spoke of holy women. It is the duty of each one of us to be a holy woman. We shall have elevated aims, if we are holy women. We shall feel that we are called to perform important duties. No one is exempt from them. There is no sister so isolated, and her sphere so narrow but what she can do a great deal towards establishing the Kingdom of God upon the earth. * * *

God bless you, my sisters, and encourage you, that you may be filled with light . . . inasmuch as you are rht.

wise stewards, you will find time for social duties, because these are incumbent upon us as daughters and mothers in Zion. By seeking to perform every duty you will find that your capacity will increase, and you will be astonished at what you can accomplish. . . . You, my sisters, if you are faithful will become **Queens of Queens, and Priestesses unto the Most High God.** *These are your callings. We have only to discharge our duties. By and by our labors will be past, and our names will be crowned with everlasting honor, and be had in everlasting remembrance among the Saints of the Most High God. (***Women's Exponent***, Vol. 2, Sept. 1873)*

John Taylor had a great appreciation for his sister Saints and paid the following tribute to them:

Now, crowns, thrones, exaltations and dominions are in reserve for thee in the eternal worlds, and the way is opened for thee to return back into the presence of thy Heavenly Father, if thou wilt only **abide by and walk in a celestial law, fulfil the designs of thy creation, and hold out to the end.** *That when mortality is laid in the tomb, you may go down to your grave in peace, arise in glory, and receive your everlasting reward in the resurrection of the just, along with thy head and husband. Thou wilt be permitted to pass by the Gods and angels who guard the gates, and onward, upward to thy exaltation in a celestial world among the Gods. To be a priestess queen unto thy Heavenly Father, and a glory to thy husband and offspring, to bear the souls of men, to people other worlds, (as thou didst bear their tabernacles in mortality,) while eternity goes and eternity comes; and if you will receive it, lady, this is eternal life. And herein is the saying of the Apostle Paul fulfilled, "that the man is not without the woman, neither the woman without the man, in the Lord." (I Cor. 11:11) "That man is the head of the woman, and the glory of the man is the woman." (I Cor. 11:7) Hence, thine origin, the object of thy creation, and* *thy ultimate destiny, if faithful. Lady, the cup is within thy reach; drink then the heavenly draught, and live. (**The Mormon**, Aug. 29, 1857)*

The path to exaltation is straight and narrow, but the promised blessings, powers, and glories of heaven are attainable. In their fullness, they can be received only through the marriage of a righteous man and woman (women) as they share those covenants in the Holy Priesthood.

If a woman wants to hold the Priesthood, she should be married to a man who holds and honors it. If she is married to a man who does not have it, she should help him acquire it. Today the true Priesthood is hard to find. With all the sins of the Saints, changes in ordinances and ordinations, and giving Priesthood where it does not belong, the real Priesthood is becoming more and more difficult to locate. As early as 1846 Brigham Young prophesied of these present-day perils:

> *The Council requested me to give them instructions. I told them that unless this people would humble them- selves and cease their wickedness, God would not give them much more teaching nor would it be long until the Priesthood would be hunted by those who now call themselves saints. (Manuscript History of B.Y., pp. 476- 477; reprinted in Sermons and Writings, Pioneer Press, Vol. 1, p. 99)*

Men and women often try to find a short-cut method of receiving the blessings and promises of Priesthood. But the Holy Priesthood is not received by picketing, public pressures, or because of social stature, sex, or race. It is acquired through righteousness, through trial and test, and by walking the straight and narrow path of obedience to eternal laws, ordinances and principles the Lord has restored in this dispensation. President John Taylor spoke of the blessings that result from such righteous living:

Oh, if we could comprehend the glory, the intelligence, the power, the majesty and dominion of our Heavenly Father! If we could contemplate the exaltation, the glory, the happiness which awaits the righteous, the pure and the virtuous, of those who fear God, even the Saints of the Most High! If we could comprehend the great blessings that God has in store for those people that fear him and observe his laws and keep his commandments, we should feel very different from what we do. But then, we do not. The Lord has brought us from among the different nations, that we may be educated in the things of the kingdom of God. He has conferred the Holy Priesthood for that purpose. (JD 22:315-16)

* * *

Questions still remain unanswered regarding Priesthood and women's relationship to it, but we do know that a righteous LDS woman, in connection with her husband to whom she has been sealed by Priesthood authority, can enjoy the birthright, powers, blessings, rights, privileges, and gifts of the Priesthood. She is indeed the most blessed among women! As Eliza R. Snow so beautifully penned about Latter-day Saint women:

__They occupy a more important position than is occupied by any other women on the earth.__ Associated, as they are, with apostles and prophets inspired by the living God—with them __sharing in the gifts and powers of the holy Priesthood.__ . . participating in those sacred ordinances, without which, we could never be prepared to dwell in the presence of the Holy Ones. ("Position and Duties," __Woman's Exponent__ 3:28, July 15, 1874)

INDEX

C

Cadijah, mother of Mohammed, 24

Candlemass, memorial festival to Jesus, 83

Cannon, Abraham H., necessary to state Melchizedek Priesthood was conferred, 61; relates to Joseph Smith vision of Adam and Eve, 23

Card, Zina, interpreted blessings in tongues, 148

Catholic Church, status on Mary more than Christ, 84; had a woman pope for two years, 84, prays more to Mary than the Son or the Father, 84

Catholics, worshiped a mother in heaven, 82

Ceres, ancient matriarch who was worshiped, 83

Chapman, J.E., was quoted in *S.L. Tribune,* in favor of women holding a Priesthood Office, 95-96

Children, "an heritage of the Lord," 15; brought to Jesus in land Bountiful, 41; "suffer the little c. to come unto me," 15
9, 12-15, 22, 41-43, 48, 52, 53, 57, 59, 66-68, 72-75, 79, 88, 89, 93, 107, 135, 139, 152, 153, 158, 162, 167, 170, 175, 177

Christ, gave Priesthood authority to 12 men, 54
13, 19, 29, 30, 40, 49, 54, 56, 57, 60, 64, 74, 81-84, 94, 95, 98, 114-116, 131, 135, 140, 152, 153, 157, 158, 160, 173, 175, 181

Church of Christ, should contain a Patriarch, 64

Church, LDS c. "most democratic institution in the world" (JFS), 94; LDS c. organization and gifts described by O. Pratt, 158-159
14, 17, 23, 24, 30-32, 37, 44, 45, 48, 49, 55-57, 59, 60, 62-64, 66, 69-71, 73-75, 79-87, 92-104, 107, 108, 110-116, 119-121, 123, 125, 133, 134, 139-142, 144-146, 148-151, 153, 155-162, 169, 172, 175, 177

Clark, J. Reuben, Jr., women do not receive Priesthood, 142

Clawson, Rudger, Priesthood is not held by women, 140-141

Cleveland, Sarah, called as R.S. counselor, 62

Coltrin, Zebedee, 22

Conferral of Priesthood, four questions regarding, 63-64; importance of doing properly, 59-61; wording of, 59-60

Constitution, U.S., guarantees of, 164

Coriantumr, recovered from his wounds and gathered his people, 42-43

Cornerstone, of S.L. Temple laid, 104

Covet, no one should, 15, 173

Cowdery, Oliver, 22, 59, 102

Critchlow, Wm. J., Priesthood is not conferred upon women, 143

Cullom Bill, feelings against, 164

Curse, of women, 175-179; women redeemed from, 177
7, 14, 15, 52, 138, 175-177, 179

Cyril (Bishop of alexandria), the worship of Mary should be recognized, 82

D

Daughters of Eve, third millennia unlocked to, 75

Daughters of Zion, described by Isaiah, 50-52

Deacon, 92, 156

Democratic, 94, 95

Derr, Jill Mulvay, wrote "Woman's Place in B.Y.'s World", 73-93

Desolation, city of, 43

Deseret News Press, women do not hold Priesthood, 141

Dragon, prevailed not against Michael, the child or the woman, 56 89

Draper, John W., historian, controvoersy over worshipping the Mother of God, 82

E

East, Mrs, Wilmarth, speaker at 1870 mass meeting, 163

Economy of Heaven, 9

Elder, a necessary appendage belonging to high priesthood, 92
7, 14, 15, 52, 138, 175-177, 179

Elders, to be called to anoint with oil JFS), 157
39, 47, 60, 84, 129, 132, 138-140

N

O

P

grand orders of Priesthood, 64; will continue throughout eternity, 22, 179

22, 64, 65, 120, 170, 179

Paul, advised women to wear modest apparel, 31; likened the church to human body, 97; placed speaking restrictions on women in the church, 31, 101; recognized necessary labors of women in the church, 30; said, "Neither is the man without the women...", 113, 183; said women would be saved in the childbearing, 31; talked about "one flesh", 131-132; told about Philip's four daughters who prophesied, 30-31

7, 30, 31, 45, 53, 97, 101, 113, 131, 141, 158, 159, 175, 182, 183

Pearl, the, an early Christian writing, 89

Pearson, Carol Lynn, author of "Healing the motherless Home", 75; took up banner for women's rights, 74-75

Penrose, Charles Wo., a nation of kings and priests, 118; sisters are not ordained to any office in the Priesthood, 140

Peter, gave suggestions to wives and husbands, 32-33

29, 32, 33

Phebe, commended by Paul, 30

Philip, the evangelist and father of four daughters, 30

Plural Marriage, supported by 5000-6000 women in 1870 mass meetings, 161-170

111, 123, 161

Pope Joan, under disguise of a man, was a pope for two years, 84

Pratt, Orson, common in O.T. for women to receive revelation, 148; described organization and gifts of true Church of Jesus Christ, 158-159; described power of Priesthood, 126-127

Presentation of Mary, a festival initiated after 9th century, 83

Priestess, a female Priest, 119

109, 113, 115-117, 119, 136, 138, 142, 146, 147, 183

Priesthood, acquired through righteousness, 184; authority and p. are

two different things, 63; conferral of, 59-61; definitions of, 46-47, 49 fullness of p. cannot be reached without women, 174; greater than the Church, 93; has become chief idol of modern church, 49; how p. should be maintained, 65; is necessary to receive temple endowment, 106; Israel unworthy of p., 118; keys of p. always held by men, 53; lesser p. continued when Moses and Holy Priesthood were taken away, 107; man holding p. may have no office in the church, 102; not found without righteous principles, 29; perfect law of theocracy (JS), 119; power extends beyond the grave, 113; power necessary to enter the presence of God, 113; received by Adam in pre-mortal world, 10; relationship of women to, 45; should be honored 52; today's conditions lead women away from p., 58; true p. is hard to find today, 184; twelve reasons why men have dominion in p., 54; women can't be deprived of blessings, powers and privileges of p., 44; women hold p. in connection with husbands, 134-139 would be hunted by so-called Satins (BY), 184

7, 10, 17, 18, 21, 23, 24, 28, 29, 32, 33, 44-55, 57-66, 68-70, 73-75, 84, 87, 92-100, 102, 103, 105-127, 129-148, 150, 151, 153, 155-158, 161, 171-174, 178, 184, 185

Priestly authority, described by O. Pratt, 126-127

Priscilla, Paul's Helper, 30

Prophetess, examples of, 25

25, 101, 125, 146, 147

Q

Queen, definition of, 119-120, 128; in second anointings, 115-129; 138, 143, 183; shares responsibilities, callings and powers with her king, 127

34-37, 81, 87, 88, 109, 113, 115-117,

T

does not receive Priesthood during endowment (HCK), 108, 116-117; essential to the image of god, 13; first to whom Christ appeared after His death, 13; from Syro-Phoenicia, 29; gave the world the Savior, 7; has her free agency 57; has not right to found a church (JS), 101; holds Priesthood in conjunction with her husband, 116-117, 150; made for the man, 20-21; "made of a rib...to be equal with him", 19; mother of the world, 71; no great principle has been revealed to LDS Church through w., (JFS), 99; not to be followed as a leader by servants of God (BY), 102; not to dictate the husband (BY), 93; receives Mel. Prstd. when she receives endowment (Quinn), 103, 114; restricted to that level of Priesthood held by her husband, 145; shares in Priesthood rights, powers, privileges and blessings, 65, 132; term used for Eve in Genesis, 11; virtuous w. described by Solomon, 13; well defined in Mormon temple, 119; with man in the creation, 13 7, 11-13, 16-21, 23, 24, 28-31, 33-36, 44-46, 48, 50, 54-58, 63, 65-68, 70-72, 74-77, 84, 93, 96, 98-103, 106, 108, 112, 113, 117, 119-121, 125, 128, 129, 131-133, 135, 138, 141, 142, 144-148, 150, 153, 156, 157, 164, 165, 167-169, 173-185

Woman's Exponet, 71-72

Women, are not shown proper respect and love, 51, 71; being taught self-dependence, 76; can't be deprived of blessings, powers and privileges of Priesthood, 44; can't hold Priesthood apart from their husbands (BY), 48; considered prophetesses in Book of Mormon, 44; could also enjoy spiritual gifts (JS), 150-151; encouraged by BY to develop talents outside the home, 73; experienced spiritual outpourings and even went to battle (against Lamanites), 42-43; do not have Priesthood, 139-143; first oat the tomb and to witness the risen Lord, 30; followed Jesus on HIs last jour-

ney to Jerusalem and His crucifixion, 30; giving blessings, 148; God worked through w. anciently, 26; Greater numbers of w. exalted than men, 174; have stronger moral inclinations (BY), 50; in subjection to their husbands, 33; many w. are smarter than their husbands (BY), 50; men should be considerate of w., 48; nature of, 49-53; not actually the weaker sex, 49; not called to function in Church Priesthood offices, 44; not placed to lead, but to be led (HCK), 47-48; not to be worshiped, 87-88; often superior in spiritual things, 50; prepared christ's body for burial, 30; protected by God from coming under curse of not honoring Priesthood, 52; question of what authority of w. hold, 94; roles of, 56; "rule over them", (Isaiah), 48; saved in child-bearing, 31; selected w. had same freedoms and privileges of the king in ancient Israel, 26; share the authority of the Priesthood with their husbands, 112-113, 119, 133-139, 185; should not wash and anoint women who are sick (JFS), 157; 60% of w. in Utah work, 76; some w. want Priesthood conferred with subsequent Priesthood ordination, 95; source of w. is the Priesthood (HCK), 53; strong-minded w. make best helpmeets for their husbands, 76; unfair and unequal treatment of wo. is diminishing, 77; used as spiritual examples by Jesus, 30 7, 12-14, 17, 18, 21, 22, 24-27, 29-34, 36, 37, 40, 42-45, 47-52, 54-59, 62, 63, 65, 66, 68-79, 81, 86, 87, 90, 93-101, 103, 108-114, 118-120, 125, 128, 130, 131, 133-137, 139-145, 147-150, 153-158, 160-162, 165-169, 171, 172, 174-179, 182, 184, 185

Women of Mormondom, (Tullidge), gives respect to Eve and her mission, 21

Women's rights, 77, 78

Woodruff, Phoebe, speaker at 1870 mass meeting, 169-170

Woodruff, Wilford, defines Priesthood, 46

Y

Young, Brigham, counsels sisters to
obey their husbands, but not follow
them to the devil, 57; defines
Priesthood, 46; encouraged sisters
to administer to the sick, 152;
encouraged women to develop talents outside the home, 72-73;
explains curse upon women, 175-
177; explains duties of women in
relation to the Priesthood, 66-67,
129; lenient and understanding
toward Adam and Eve, 9; mystery
why God allowed Lucifer to tempt
Eve, 8; opinion of women's rights
gets more liberal, 72; Priesthood
would be hunted by future Saints,
184; received second anointings
(with Mary Ann Young), 115-116,
126; sermon at the laying of S.L.
Temple cornerstone, 104-107;
woman has her free agency, 57;
women are entitled to the kingdom
and exaltation, 57; women are
more ready to love the right than
men, 50; women don't hold
Priesthood apart from their husbands, 48; women have no right to
meddle in Kingdom of God, 48,
135; women have stronger moral
inclinations, 50

Z

Zondervan, B. D., Scholar and publisher, 13; woman as female counterpart is essential to image of God, 13
Zondervan Encyclopedia of the Bible,
13, 30

BOOKS WRITTEN OR COMPILED BY
OGDEN KRAUT